Proven flies for the Pacific Northwest

DON HAAHEIM

Cataloguing data available from Library and Archives Canada
978-0-88839-768-3 [paperback]
978-0-88839-771-3 [epub]

Printed in South Korea

We acknowledge the support of the Government of Canada through the Canada Book Fund and the Canada Council for the Arts, and of the Province of British Columbia through the British Columbia Arts Council and the Book Publishing Tax Credit.

Hancock House gratefully acknowledges the Halkomelem Speaking Peoples whose unceded, shared and asserted traditional territories our offices reside upon.

Published simultaneously in Canada and the United States by
HANCOCK HOUSE PUBLISHERS LTD.
19313 Zero Avenue, Surrey, B.C. Canada V3Z 9R9
#104-4550 Birch Bay-Lynden Rd, Blaine, WA, U.S.A. 98230-9436
(800) 938-1114 Fax (800) 983-2262
www.hancockhouse.com info@hancockhouse.com

Contents

Dedication

This book is dedicated to fishermen and women everywhere who truly enjoy the rapture of casting an artificial fly of their own making on beckoning waters well away from those daily life stresses! And also to my family for putting up with my devout enthusiasm for all aspects of fly fishing for these many, fun-filled years!

Introduction

I grew up on a small dairy farm in South Langley, then a rural part of British Columbia's Fraser Valley. Very luckily for me, as an only child, my father, Olaf Haaheim, was an avid outdoorsman. He always endeavored, even when I was very young, to include me in his outdoor adventures, whether it was spring-time fishing in the Little Campbell Creek that ran through our farm, or fall hunting for ducks, pheasants and grouse, with an occasional deer thrown in! Besides his everyday dairy farm chores, my father also ran a registered seasonal trap line along three miles of the Little Campbell, and I often accompanied him on his trap rounds. Fortunately, my mother, Alice, an excellent wild game cook, seemed to understand the joy I found in sharing outdoor time with my father. Consequently, my early years are filled with many wonderful outdoor memories!

My first recollection of fishing was in a willow-lined pool in the Little Campbell Creek accessed by a huge fir log that old-time loggers had cut. By mistake, it had fallen directly into the thick, hardtack willow brush that profusely grew on both sides of the creek channel. The tree span was so long that that it reached almost 100 feet out to the main creek bed, where a nice pool about 20 feet wide formed just in front of an old beaver dam. The log base was roughly 6 feet in diameter, so steps were built to climb on top of the gigantic old timber, which sloped downward into the creek at about a five-degree angle. I can remember as a young lad feeling butterflies in my stomach every time I followed my father along that log walkway to the enticing pool at the end.

We did not use flies in those days but rather long willow sticks, cut near streamside, with green cutty-hunk line tied directly to the end of the pole! A bare hook baited with an earthworm was standard fare for cutthroat trout of 10 to 12 inches in length that frequented our section of the Little Campbell every spring in April and May. In those years there was also an abundance of small coho salmon some 3 to 4 inches long that eagerly snapped at our bait, but my father ensured that all of these delicate fish were returned unharmed to the water. A very occasional steelhead of much larger size found its way up to our property, but they mostly resided a few miles closer to the Little Campbell outlet at White Rock, where the stream bottom contained much more sand and gravel.

I recall buying my first fly rod with berry-picking money when I was 11 years old, a white Shakespeare model of early fiberglass construction. My casting then was very much of "cut and try," but soon I found a way to cast a fly around 20 or 30 feet to small open-water pools often ringed with lily pads and thick willows, at least on one side of the creek. The flies I used were purchased from Bishop's Sports Shop in Langley or very cheap imported fly packages sold by the Army and Navy store in New Westminster. Typical were Parmachene Belles, Royal Coachmans, Grizzly Kings, Silver Doctors and the like. No matter, the small coho were always ready to strike, and although seldom caught, they provided much exciting encouragement for me to continue. An occasional cutthroat trout did take my fly offering, and this only added to my growing zest for fly fishing! Later while in high school, I had a wonderful opportunity to attend fly casting lessons in our school gym, sponsored by the local Rod and Gun Club. I managed to quickly pick up on many subtle things that I was lacking in my previous self-taught method of casting a fly. What fun it was!

My zest for fishing was greatly enhanced when, at the tender age of 16, I purchased my first car with money earned from various labor-intensive jobs at neighboring farms, such as turkey and mink ranches. Never mind that the vehicle was over 20 years old with many miles already accumulated! This automobile, a '33 Chevy coupe with a rumble seat, gave me a huge opportunity to expand my fishing horizons, mostly in the Fraser Valley due to the excessive age of my car. During those years, coho salmon in the fall still ran in good numbers in Fraser Valley streams such as the Nicomekl and, of course, the Little Campbell. Steelhead, too, could be found in reasonable numbers in winter and early spring. While my expertise at catching these bigger trophies was limited, I did manage to land an occasional few using a cast fly, and any fish hooked with a fly continued to be a joy!

Following my high school graduation, I decided to study engineering at UBC, not realizing how much hard work that task would be! However, I did manage to obtain a degree in electrical engineering, and after graduation, I was fortunate to have three employment offers, two in Eastern Canada and the third in Vancouver. I opted for a position with BC Telephone, not that I was sure that they were superior to the other companies, but because it meant that I could continue to enjoy the wonderful outdoor opportunities in British Columbia during weekends and holidays. BC Telephone did turn out to be an excellent company. In my case, this job covered many BC locations such as downtown Vancouver, Whalley, New Westminster, Kamloops, Prince George on two different occasions, and finally, Kelowna, where I now live after more than a 30-year work career. But I am getting ahead of my intent to provide you with more insight on how I became a dedicated fly tier to go with my constant enjoyment of fly casting for all types of sport fishing.

It happened one winter when I volunteered evenings and weekends as a North Shore Winter Club minor hockey coach. A freak accident while running a hockey practice resulted in a broken kneecap, which put me in a plaster cast for six weeks, foot to thigh. Thereby encumbered with crutches for mobility, I noticed an advertisement for a fly tying course at the Vancouver Technical School. I decided that, rather than moping about my condition, I would enroll in the course, something I had wanted to do for years but always had the excuse, "Too busy now!" The course instructor was Earl Anderson, who I later found was well known for creating such flies as the Anderson Stone Nymph, the What Else Coho fly and several other patterns. I view my broken kneecap as a small blessing, because thanks to Earl's enthusiastic teaching, I learned a gratifying lifetime hobby that has given me so many rewards. I have never sold a fly but have probably given away hundreds to friends and streamside acquaintances—always a good feeling! Those of you who are already practiced fly tiers can testify to the heightened joy of catching a fish on a fly of your own making! Besides the welcome therapy of "creating" at your fly tying bench, by carrying a case of fly tying materials streamside, you can build a fly right there to "match the hatch," a feeling that can only be described as "priceless"! Enough said.

Now let's look at some of the many flies that I can guarantee will catch fish, not only in my home province of British Columbia, but I am sure in many fishing meccas throughout this wide wonderful world!

Chapter 1:

KEEP THE BASICS SIMPLE!

My fly tying mentor, Earl Anderson, continually stressed, "Keep things simple!" A new fly tier can easily be overwhelmed by the proliferation of items and gear that can be used to create artificial flies. The first thing that Mr. Anderson taught his class of "newbies" was that, while there are many devices that can enhance fly tying, not all are really needed. I clearly recall that he emphasized that only two tools were necessary, namely a sturdy fly tying vise, to hold a fishing hook firmly in place, and scissors to cut thread. Of course, one must recognize that numerous materials are required to create an artificial fly, such as hooks, tying thread, plus tail, body, hackle and wing building items, including floss, wool, chenille, fur, and feathers. Yes, there are countless items, both natural and artificial, that can be used to make a fishing lure! But before we explore the expansive world of tools and materials for fly tying—items that keep many retail shops in business—let's start with Earl Anderson's principle of keeping things simple.

A solid vise of a simple open/close design for firmly holding your hook in place is the first requirement. See Diagram 1, Basic Fly Tying Tools, on the following page. Scissors (2nd item to the right) for trimming materials and cutting tying thread are a must as well. I use a bobbin (item 3 and 4 to the right of the vise) for the convenience of holding a spool of tying thread, but Earl professed that they are not absolutely necessary. He simply taught us to push the thread through the center of the spool and let it dangle a couple of feet below your vise, thus putting some weight and therefore tension on the tying thread! In other words, tie both wraps and half hitches with your fingers rather than using tools. However, if you do not use a bobbin, you must learn how to make a half hitch primarily with one hand. To me, this is key for successful fly tying, as you can tie half hitches throughout the construction of your fly, thus making it stronger, tighter and much less likely to unravel when attacked by ravenous fish! The majority use a bobbin close to the fly for making their wraps with the tying thread and then finish the fly with a whip finisher. But Earl claimed that such a fly would come apart much easier than one made with his method of wrapping tying thread under tension by hand (thumb and index finger) with frequent half hitches made throughout the fly's construction.

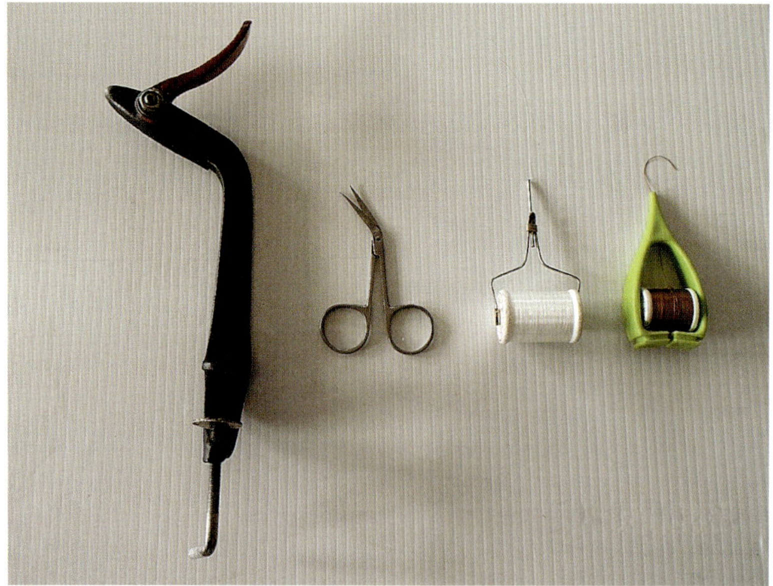

Diagram 1: Basic Fly Tying Tools: Vise, Scissors, Bobbins

Diagram 2 shows a few other tools that can make the process of fly creation easier. Included are, left to right: hackle pliers, a homemade dubbing tool, a bodkin or needle, and finishing cement—in the example shown, a "hard as nails" fingernail enamel. Other tools, such as hair stackers, whip finishers, bobbin threaders, fur combs, bee's wax, etc., are available at most fly shops, but I personally do not make much use of these items. In this book we will adopt Earl Anderson's method, using only the basics and the one-hand half hitch as explained in Chapter 2.

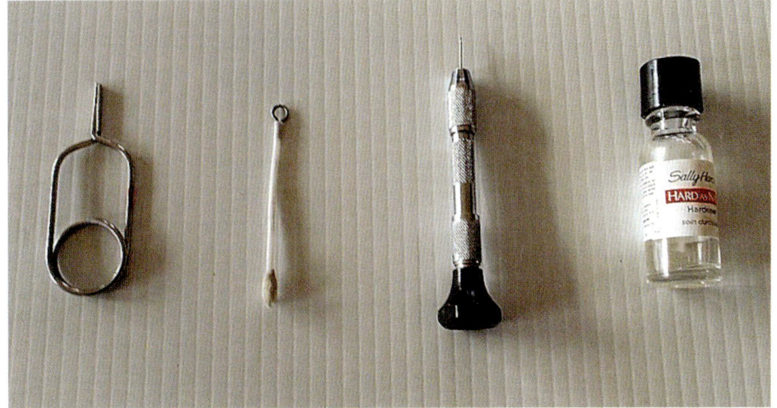

Diagram 2: Hackle Pliers, Dubbing Tool, Bodkin, Cement

Chapter 2:

THE ONE-HAND HALF HITCH & THE HAND TIED WHIP FINISH

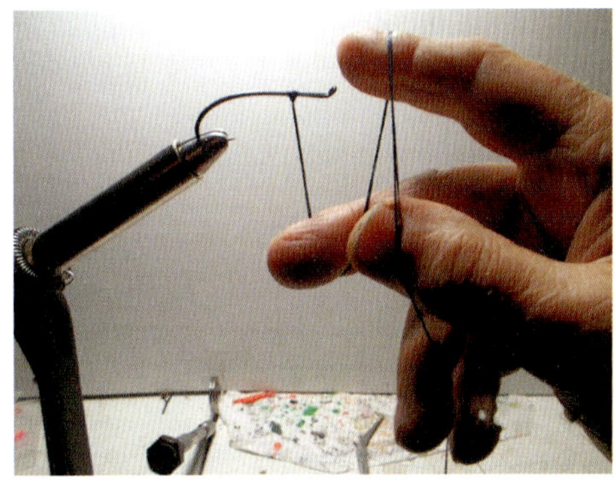

Figure 1: Secure Thread to Hook, Then Over, Under, Under the Thread

The advantage of learning the one-hand half hitch (where a finger on the other hand is used to hold the knot in place while the operating hand pulls the knot tight) is that, anywhere or any time in the fly construction, you can make a quick half hitch, thus providing durability and strength to the finished fly. A key is the tying thread must be under tension; in other words, weight must be provided by the thread spool/bobbin hanging a foot or two below the hook.

Let us start by assuming you are right-handed and you place the hook in your vise with the hook bend facing left, the hook eye to your right. With tension on the tying thread, there are three steps to make a half hitch: the first two are with your right hand, and the last step uses a left-hand finger to keep the knot in place while you pull tight with the right hand. Sound confusing? Not really; once you get the process down, it becomes automatic and extremely fast!

The first step in Figure 1 is to secure the tying thread firmly to the hook shank. With a couple of feet of length to the spool/bobbin, and a left-hand grip on the loose end, make a few wraps with your right hand, the last ones covering the initial wraps, then half hitch firmly at least twice, or simply hold the wraps tight with a left finger. Now, with your right-hand fingers spread, as in Figure 1, place your second or longest finger over the thread, fairly near to the hook shank; next, put your index finger under the thread and lift up; now allow the thread to flow over your thumb and down over your third finger to the spool/bobbin. If you are doing this for the first time, do not be tempted to guide the thread with your left hand; do it all with right-hand finger movement. Do note that there must be tension (weight) on the thread, otherwise this process is difficult to accomplish with only one hand!

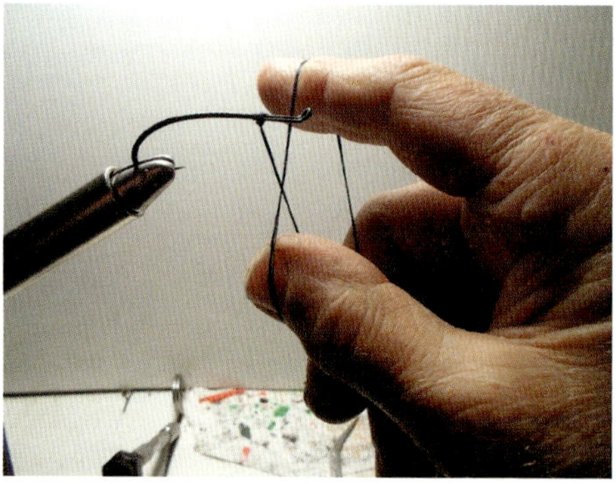

Once the thread is in place as shown, step 2 is simply a wrist turn to move the thread running between your index finger and thumb behind the hook shank, at the point where it is attached. See Figure 2 for a visual of this step.

Figure 2: Twist Wrist to Move Thread Behind the Hook Shank

Then quickly move your left index finger and press down here. Finally, roll your wrist again to the left and complete the half hitch by pulling the thread tight with your right hand. After a while, the process becomes so automatic that you can complete a half hitch in about a second! See Figure 3 for this final step.

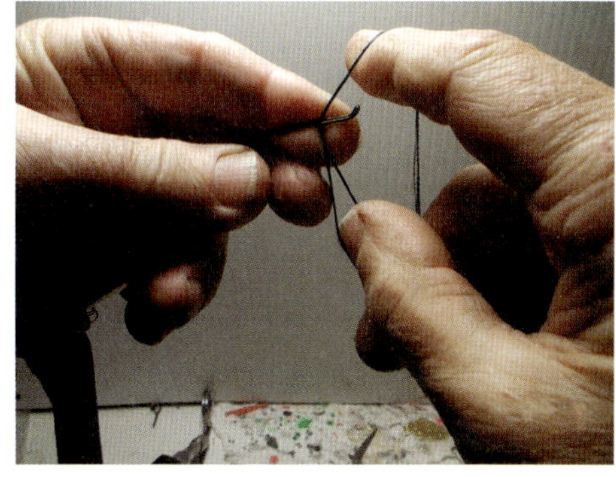
Figure 3: Left finger in Place, Pull Thread with Right Hand to Complete

The thread in both figures shown is far thicker than normal tying thread for better visibility. Tying threads are available in a vast assortment of colors and sizes. However, while working in Prince George, a wonderful tip came my way from fellow Polar Coachmen Fly Club members. It was to use invisible thread, widely used in the clothing industry. This is for a couple of excellent reasons. First, it is strong, and second, you can back wrap on your body material or a palmered hackle with very little distortion or color change to the fly, but at the same time, you are greatly strengthening the fly! I use invisible thread for 90% of my fly tying, although I have recently found that mending or invisible thread purchased at sewing shops is getting so weak that it breaks far too easily! My solution of late is to buy .006 diameter or even ultra fine monofilament, available in sewing type spools at specialized fly shops such as Trout Water Fly and Tackle.

Fly shop retailers love to sell you on whip finishers to complete a fly. Many people teach fly tying using only two steps of close bobbin wraps and a whip finish using a whip finisher tool. My argument is that flies constructed in this manner will unravel too easily! Therefore, I let my bobbin swing below the vise, primarily for tension, and use the hand method to make frequent half hitches all throughout the fly construction. I do admit that a whip finish tool will accomplish a neat fly head finish for you, but you can also do the same thing using a two-finger operation—index and second finger of your right hand—although the left hand is needed to hold the bobbin end of the thread tight.

Start by placing the thread near the hook eye over your right-hand index and second fingers, with the palm facing you, as shown in the first picture in Table 1 below. Picture 2 shows a counter-clockwise twist with a spread and raise of the second finger, placing the bobbin end thread under the thread from the hook eye. Picture 3 guides the bobbin end of the thread tight against the hook eye, where you want the whip finish. Picture 4 shows a lift of both fingers above the hook eye with a counter-clockwise twist. Picture 5 repeats the finger twist under, then behind the hook eye each time. The last picture shows, after 4 or 5 twists, the left hand pulling the loop made by the right-hand fingers tight! Ensure you do not lose the loop as you pull your right-hand fingers free and switch a finger to hold the loop in place!

Many fly tying instruction books and videos teach a bobbin wrap very close to the fly under construction and a whip finish with a Matarelli, Thompson or other similar whip finishing tools. The advantage of this method is speed, and it is most often used by commercial fly tiers. However, I prefer the Earl Anderson approach of tight finger-guided wraps, with the thread under a bit of weight tension and frequent right-hand half hitches throughout the construction process. I believe, while this takes a bit longer to do, the fly will not unravel as easily when in use. I will leave it to you to decide on your preferred method!

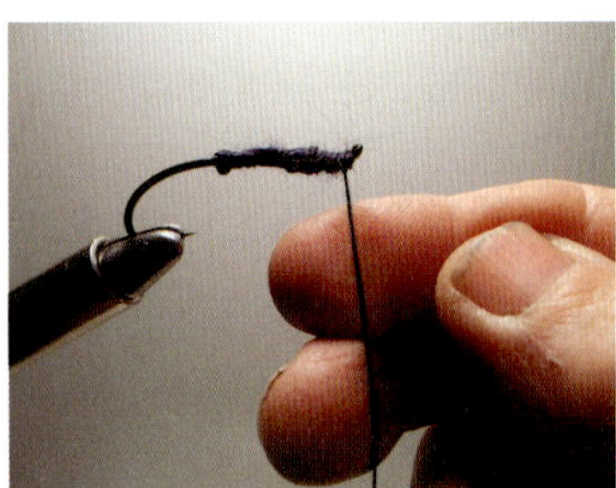

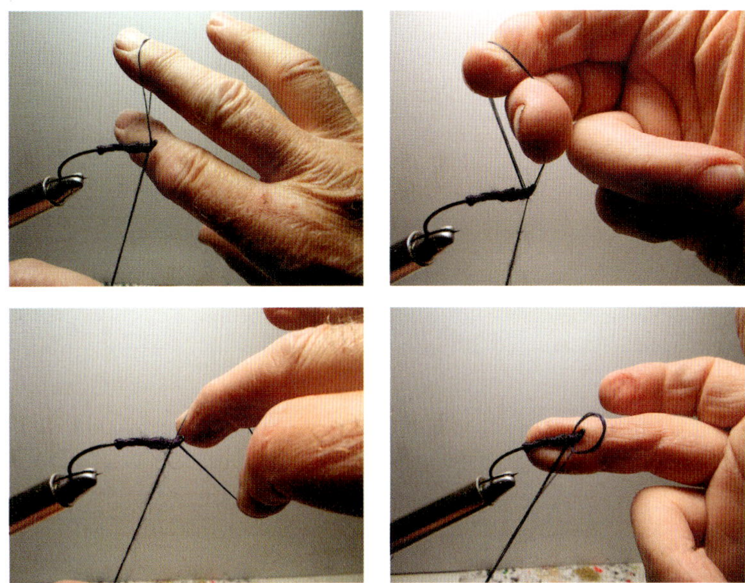

Table 1: Pictures Showing How to Make a Whip Finish by Hand

Chapter 3:

BASIC FLY TYING MATERIALS

A complete book could be written about the wealth of fly tying materials, both natural and artificial, that are available today. It is not my purpose to go into detail about all the wonderful items for fly tying that good fly shops carry, but rather to mention a few basic materials that can be used to tie literally hundreds of different fly patterns. My abbreviated list includes:

- Pheasant tail feathers
- Golden pheasant tippets
- Pheasant cape feathers
- Peacock herl
- Ostrich herl of various dyed colors
- Duck flank feathers, including mallard and wood duck
- Game hen capes, including brown, black, grizzly and badger
- Hackle feathers of many colors
- Guinea hen feathers
- Turkey tail feathers
- Goose wing feathers of various colors
- Stripped goose quills or biots
- Marabou feathers in all colors
- Dubbing blends
- Squirrel tails including grey, black and brown

- Rabbit fur strips of various colors
- Deer, elk, bear, moose and other animal hair and furs
- Calf tail in many colors
- Wool in many colors
- Mohair in many colors
- Chenille and sparkle chenille in various sizes and colors
- Tinsel: gold, silver, copper, green and red
- Crystal flash, flashabou, angel hair and many others
- Midge tubing, swannundaze and many stretch materials
- Liquid lace material, hollow, flat and round, all sizes
- Beads, both glass and metal, in various sizes
- Foam sheets for cutting into strips
- Holographic sparkle, frostbite, poly-flash in many colors
- Floss, many colors
- Yarn, many colors
- Braids, many colors
- Lead wire
- Threads, various colors and invisible mending or thin monofilament
- Hooks, many sizes, for chironomid, nymph, wet, streamer and dry flies

The list could go on and on, especially with the new synthetic materials now available with sparkle, glo and pearlescent sheens, but with just a few of the basic materials listed above, hundreds of great fish catching flies can be created!

If you are brand new to the exciting hobby of fly tying, I now must apologize, as I will not go into details of how to construct the various segments such as tail, body, wings, and hackles of a fishing fly. For the beginner, there are many excellent books and Internet sites explaining basic fly construction. My prime purpose was to promote my mentor, Earl Anderson's approach to fly tying by keeping things simple with a minimum of tools. You will also notice, as we examine my fly patterns in this book, how I absolutely prefer tying with invisible mending thread or fine monofilament and only use regular colored thread for a few of my flies! Allow me to proceed with a fly tying series beginning with chironomids, followed by wet fly patterns, including nymphs, then steelhead/salmon flies, and concluding with some of my favorite dry fly patterns. As mentioned, the pattern instructions assume that you already know the basics of fly tying.

Chapter 4:

HOW TO TIE MY FAVORITE CHIRONOMIDS

Fly 1: The Valentine Lake Chironomid

A recent July 1st weekend found us once again at our Canim Lake summer camp, which is about 38 kilometers east of the rural town of 100 Mile House. Of the many good fly fishing lakes in the 100 Mile area, Valentine Lake is a favorite! The weather had just turned sunny and warm, so what more excuse did I need to try for some of those large rainbows that lurk in Valentine Lake?

That day, my usually reliable Valentine Lake Sedge and also my Caddis Crawler did not produce any strikes in the usual spots near the BC Forest launch site. However, I noticed that a fisherman anchored in a pontoon boat in deeper water a fair distance from shore was having periodic success fishing a chironomid. I quietly moved my U-tube a bit closer and politely asked what he was using. He then generously shared information not only on the chironomid color (maroon), but also a very critical fact that the trout were not hitting anywhere near the surface but were deep, at 25 to 30 feet! This fact changed my luck around completely, with several rainbows hooked in the 18- to 20-inch range! Yes, it is more difficult to cast with a very long leader, especially if you are using a large moveable strike indicator, but I found a cast, cross wind, allowed the fly and long leader to billow out with the wind and not tangle. My experience here showed that fish are often deeper than you might expect, and a long leader with the right fly is positively the answer. Allow me to share these details with you.

Materials

- Hook – Scud size 12 to 16
- Tail – None
- Body – Burgundy wool or micro tubing
- Rib – Thin white thread
- Hackle – None
- Head – Small 7/64 gold or silver bead
- Wing – None
- Collar – A few turns of dark olive rubber super floss
- Gill – Extension of the white thread rib
- Thread – Invisible mending or thin monofilament

Instructions

Crimp the hook barb and slide the bead to the hook eye. Next, attach a length of thin white thread to the hook shank and let it extend well past the hook bend. Make the body by very tightly wrapping a very thin piece of burgundy wool or stretchy purple micro tubing hook bend to the bead. Follow this up by winding the white thread in spaced turns also to the bead to form the rib. However, do not trim it at this point but allow the thread to project just past the bead. The final step is to make a collar with several turns of dark olive super floss just behind the bead, taking care not to disturb the white thread left over the bead. Now you can trim the white thread quite short. Cement, tie off and you have finished a Valentine Lake chironomid!

The West End of Valentine Lake

Fly 2: The Gardom Lake Chironomid

While fishing with chironomids can be very exciting, it can also be frustrating when you cannot find the color or size of chironomid that the trout are taking! I am often surprised at the range of colors that will at times produce strikes. If you travel north from my home in Kelowna, through Vernon and then up the long hill at the turn-off to Salmon Arm just past Enderby, you will find the Gardom Lake access road at the top of the hill. This lake is fast becoming a favorite chironomid lake for me! On an earlier trip, another frequent lake visitor, Roy Williams, reported that a white chironomid with black ribbing seemed to be a winner. Sure enough, it does work, so let's have a close look at the recipe for tying this fly.

Materials

- Hook – Scud size 10 to 14
- Body – White Uni-floss or glo yarn
- Rib – Thin black plastic thread
- Head – Small blue or black bead
- Collar – Peacock herl
- Gills – Soft white Uni-floss or glo yarn
- Thread – Invisible mending or thin monofilament

Instructions

Pinch the barb of the curved scud hook and slip the bead through to the fly eye. I then like to make a few wraps of thin lead wire just behind the bead, as most of my fish hook-ups occur near the lake bottom. Next, attach a length of thin, shiny black thread to the hook shank prior to wrapping the body with white Uni-floss hook bend to hook eye. You can let the floss project a bit past the bead to trim later. Try to develop a body taper, thinner at the bend and larger as you approach the bead. Now tightly wind the black thread over the body in spaced turns to form a rib. The last steps are to wind a collar of peacock herl behind the bead and then cut the floss to show a short "gill" over the bead. After tying off, a coat of Sally Hansen's "Hard as Nails" hardener will ensure a nice finish to your fly!

Chironomid Alley at the West End of Gardom Lake

Fly 3: The Marquart Chironomid

The Marquart Chironomid is a fly that was almost an accident of my fly tying bench. Lundbom Lake, one of my favorite still water locations for large trout, is just over an hour's drive in a westerly direction from my home in Kelowna. A few years ago, I wanted to tie some classic chironomids for Lundbom, black with a gold wire rib and gold bead. At the time, I didn't have or rather could not find correct ingredients, so I made do with what I had on hand: silver beads and copper wire for the rib. A short time later, I found the fishing at Lundbom slow, with only one good fish landed on a leech pattern. On the way out, I noticed many enticing rises on the smaller but pretty Marquart Lake. As it was yet early in the afternoon, I slowly drove my pickup truck down to the west-side shore and unloaded my car topper once more. The trout were not as large as in neighboring Lundbom, and they appeared to be feeding on a hatch of dark chironomids. As it happened, the only black chironomid in my fly box was the silver beaded one with the copper rib! Oh well, why not give it a try? You guessed it, solid action from the word go! Enough said. So let's have a look at the fly tying bench mistake!

Materials

- Hook – Scud size 10 to 16
- Tail – None
- Body – Black wool or cord
- Rib – Copper wire
- Hackle – None

- Head – Small cyclops nickel bead
- Wing – None
- Collar – Black Hare's Ear dubbing or equivalent
- Thread – Invisible mending or thin monofilament

Instructions

I like tying chironomids on short shank scud hooks, often using a larger size, such as a 10 hook, than the naturals. Another factor about chironomids is that they are easy to tie, especially when using a hook of that size. Anyway, start this fly by slipping a cyclops nickel 7/64 or 5/64 inch bead through to the hook eye. As an option, you can add a few turns of thin lead wire just behind the bead if you desire a faster sink rate. Then secure a length of copper wire to the hook shank. Next, wrap black wool or cord material hook bend to the bead, followed by a few turns in the opposite direction with the copper wire to form the rib. The final step is to form a dubbing loop with black Hare's Ear or similar material such as mohair to make a collar or thorax just behind the bead. Tie off, cement and you have finished the Marquart Lake Chironomid!

Marquart Lake

Fly 4: The Doreen Chironomid

I seldom participate in fishing derbies because of a feeling that personal gain is often promoted over the value of the resource. However, prior to my transfer to Kelowna, a BC Telephone employee-organized fishing derby had been held for many years in the Central Okanagan. It was called the High Lakes Derby, centered at Doreen Lake just east of Winfield, BC. The derby, held on Father's Day weekend in June, was for telephone employees and retirees. A fundamental rule was that the derby had to be chaired by the previous year's winner! Amazingly enough, the derby was always successful, with prizes for all regardless if a fish was caught. My work philosophy as an Area Manager was to participate in as many employee functions as possible, so I put aside my fishing derby prejudices and entered following my transfer to Kelowna. In my 19 years of derby participation, I managed to bring home the largest trout on nine occasions, so I became quite adept at the High Lakes derby organization, at least for the 30 or more cheerful participants!

One early Saturday derby morning I was up and about early, heading to a favorite area location, Lost Lake, accompanied by my yellow Labrador, Jessie. In less than an hour, I hooked a good fish, not as large as my previous year's winner, casting a green shrimp on a sink tip line. As Lost has a one-fish limit, I immediately headed for shore, planning to do a little more fishing at our campsite lake, Doreen. As I was pulling my car topper out of the water, I met Ken, a Kelowna teacher who was quite anxious to get out on the water after a week of administering student exams. Ken very kindly gave me one of his favorite chironomids, a fly tied with #61 frostbite and ribbed with fine copper wire on a size 10 Daiichi hook. It also featured a white opaque bead at the eye and a couple of turns of brown pheasant just behind the bead. I arrived at the far end of Doreen just before noon as the wind began to blow rather strongly. Dennis Caryk was fishing with his son at that end, where he caught several fish the day before, including, as it turned out, the derby winner. I called to Dennis, asking where a good spot to anchor would be. He answered, "Right where you are!" Sure enough, a few minutes later, a fish savagely hit the chironomid Ken had given to me. Shortly after, I had another strike, so I looked over to Dennis and said, "Sure is a great spot that you recommended!" In all, I hooked nine rainbows between 12 noon and 1 p.m., all released as my fish from the morning was somewhat larger. I have since tied similar chironomids to Ken's and have been very pleased with the results at many different lakes.

Materials

- Hook – Mustad 3399A or Daiichi 1510 size 10 to 14
- Body – #61 frostbite or copper flashabou
- Ribbing – Fine copper wire
- Thorax – A few wraps of brown pheasant or dark peacock herl
- Head – Opaque white bead
- Thread – Invisible mending or thin monofilament

Instructions

First, crimp the hook barb in order to slip the bead through to the hook eye. Next, attach the copper # 61 frostbite and also the fine copper wire to the hook shank. Then, starting part way down the hook bend, wrap the copper wire as a spaced rib forward to the thorax followed by the frostbite. Just behind the bead, shape a short thorax with a few turns of brown pheasant, peacock herl or perhaps a rubbery super floss. Tie off, cement and you have finished Ken's copper chironomid, which I have found excellent in not only Doreen but many other BC lakes as well!

Doreen Lake Fishing Derby; Don kneeling left, Al Kouritzin standing right

Fly 5: The Black Chironomid

One of my favorite North Okanagan lakes is White Lake, nestled between Salmon Arm and Sorrento, BC, and just a few kilometers north of the Trans-Canada Highway. During late May and early June, chironomid hatches are plentiful, enough so that larger trout actively feed on these rather small insects, primarily near the bottom in the larva stage. I have found a plain black imitation often works well at this time of year. When the fish are fussy, a black chironomid ribbed with white is sometimes a producer, but many times, a good old "plain black" is the answer!

On a partly cloudy spring day a few years ago, I could see the occasional trout swimming near bottom in about 15 feet of water at the southwest shoal area. I anchored further out in deeper water in order to cast over the feeding fish toward shore. The action was rather slow, so I cast out my floating line with 14 feet of leader tied to a size 14 black chironomid and let the wind slowly carry the line in a wide arc over the shoal while the rod rested along the boat bottom. As I was alone in the dinghy, I grabbed my sink tip fly outfit and began casting a wet attractor fly, hoping to interest one of the large trout that occasionally cruised by.

Then it happened! The rod with the black chironomid was almost yanked out of the boat! A huge rainbow jumped some 60 feet away but still remained hooked! I scrambled to save the rod from going overboard and did nothing but hold on as the big fish made a distant run away from the car topper. Some long, exciting minutes later, a four-pound rainbow came to my net, the black chironomid still firmly in place. Let's have a look at this black chironomid fly.

Materials

- Hook--Scud size 10 to 16
- Body--Black micro tubing
- Head--Small 7/64 gold, silver or black bead
- Wing--None
- Collar--A few turns of black ostrich frond, optional white
- Thread--Invisible mending or thin monofilament

Instructions

Again, start by pinching the hook barb in order to slide a small bead through to the hook eye. Often color does not matter, but the example shown is gold. Next, tightly wrap a small, stretchy black material like liquid lace, micro tubing or swannundaze hook bend to the hook bead. Finish the fly next to the bead with a couple of turns of black ostrich frond, or as an option, white can be used. If you wish, a white gill can be added either ahead or over the bead.

White Lake near the South West Shoal

Fly 6: The Chaoborus

When we lived in Kamloops, I had the luxury of making after-work trips to nearby Jocko Lake, which was only about 30 minutes away. Jocko is an interesting lake in that often trout can be surging at the surface in huge numbers. Easy pickings? No. When this happens, rarely will either a dry or a wet fly entice strikes even though many fish are present! A Whiteshield Crescent neighbor, John Wright, who was a very experienced Kamloops-area fly fisherman, told me that the Jocko fish were feeding on chaoborus, a tiny, almost clear midge larva. He went on to say that the midge larvae are an extremely easy meal in their abundance and trout gorge themselves to the point that they will seldom strike at any other offering. I thought about this for some time and decided to try to invent an imitation of the tiny, clear chaoborus larva. After some effort, I came up with a fly that did catch a fine Jocko rainbow during one of the chaoborus feeding sprees. Did it always work? No, but I think the fly is worth having, if nothing more than to ease the frustration when actively feeding trout refuse any of your offerings!

Materials

- Hook – Partridge Klink-hamer 15BNX size 14 to 18
- Tail – None
- Body – 15 to 30 pound clear nylon fishing line
- Head – Small clear glass bead
- Thorax – Thin white ostrich herl

- Thread – Invisible mending or thin clear monofilament

Instructions

Start by crimping the hook barb and slip a small, clear glass bead through to the hook eye. Chaoborus, or midge larvae, tend to drift up and down in the water, rising slowly (an easy target for foraging trout) as evening approaches, therefore, I do not add weight to this fly. Using invisible mending thread is a necessity to tie the body, as you simply take a piece of clear nylon fishing line, straight from the bead to hook bend, and wrap it to the hook shank with the thread. The final step is to add a very thin thorax or collar of white ostrich herl just behind the bead. After tying off, place a generous amount of clear cement throughout the body to add a bit of clear bulk to it. Even though the Jocko Lake chaoborus larvae that I observed were transparent, with small black internal spots head and tail, my midge larva imitation will sometimes catch trout when they are on a chaoborus feeding spree!

A Typical Merritt–Kamloops Plateau Lake

Fly 7: The Dugan Red Chironomid

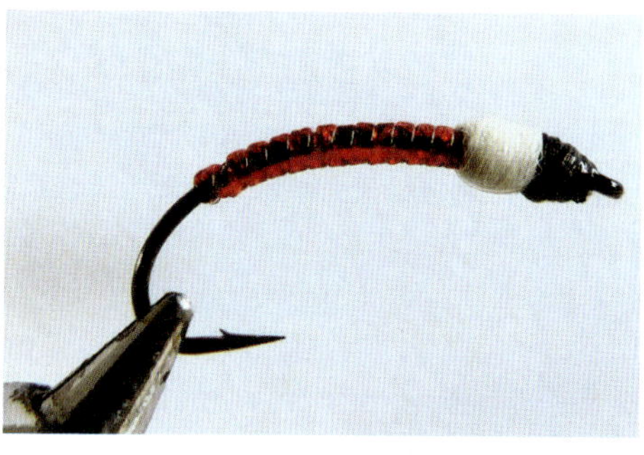

Dugan Lake is a very exciting Central Cariboo lake located a few kilometers up the Horsefly Road. This route starts at the north end of the small truck stop called 150 Mile House, a name originating from the gold rush days of the last century. Except for the last 200 yards, the road is paved all the way, a delight for family vehicles! Now

Dugan features some outstanding chironomid fishing both spring and fall. An exciting fact about this lake is that it contains both brook and rainbow trout, some growing to hefty sizes. Both parking and overnight camping can be found at this lake, although when the hatches are on, it can be a very popular place.

On a recent trip to Dugan, I did not spend a lot of time exploring the lake but rather fished close by the car top launch spot. I was advised to try either red or black chironomids, so I decided right off to go with red. I was not disappointed, as several trout were caught and released, including one nice brookie. The big fish that I was hoping to keep for the table never did materialize, but I was still happy with my outing. The fly that worked well was a red chironomid that we will now examine.

Materials

- Hook – Partridge Klink-hamer 15BNX size 16
- Body – Thin red vinyl stretch material
- Thorax – White Uni-floss
- Head – Black olive super floss

- Thread – Invisible mending or fine monofilament

Instructions

The key to this fly is to use very thin red stretch material such as vinyl ribbing. I tightly tie the end of the red vinyl at the fly head, working it straight back along the hook shank just past the bend. Then, with very tight turns, I wind the tubing forward and tie off at the hook eye. Next, make a few turns of the white Uni-floss fairly close to the hook eye, but leave room for a head. The head is wrapped with a few turns of dark super floss. An option is a bead head. Cement, tie off and you have made the Dugan Lake fly!

Dugan Lake, looking north from the launch ramp

Fly 8: The Chromie

Over the years I have found that fishing has many benefits besides catching fish! Just to be outside, close to nature, can be awesome, and you will find that most people who ply fishing rods on lakes or rivers are really fine individuals once you get to know them! A good example is my Seattle friend, Steve Clements, who regularly fishes Quesnel's Dragon Lake. Steve has not missed a spring season on Dragon Lake for many years, and in this time period, he has met many of the Dragon Lake regulars.

Need I say that Dragon Lake supports some enormous rainbow trout, a fitting challenge for dedicated fly fishermen! Such friends are Keith and Cleo Findley, who have kindly provided me with a terrific chironomid pattern with undeniable proof that it works! Keith's fly is called the "Chromie," a chironomid originally developed by Philip Rowley, who is a regular fly tying contributor to a fine British Columbia fishing and hunting magazine, *BC Outdoors*. Why am I excited about the Chromie? Well, Keith just happened to land and release one of those monster Dragon rainbows on a size 14 Chromie! Even more special, Keith's wife Cleo was able to take a photo of the giant fish, one of the best live fish pictures I have ever seen, before the rainbow was placed back in the lake unharmed. Let's have a look at Philip Rowley's fly, as tied by Keith Findley.

Materials

- Hook – Dai-Riki #135 size 14
- Tail – None
- Hackle – None
- Body – Silver holographic mylar
- Rib – Small red ultra wire
- Gills – White sparkle yarn, option white antron
- Head – Small black metal bead
- Thorax – Black/brown thread, option stripped peacock herl
- Thread – Black Uni size 0/8

Instructions

Debarb the hook and install the black bead. After securing the hook in your vise, tie in a small clump of gill material near the hook eye. The clump must be small enough for the bead to slide over the gill material as you snug the bead up to the hook eye. Then trim the gills as needed a bit past the hook eye. Next, tie in your thread just past the bead and form a base to the mid hook bend. Return the thread to the bead and tie in the silver mylar plus the red wire. Now wind the thread back to the hook bend and return to the bead. This will better secure the body material and make a very slight taper of the body – but do keep the body slender!

The next step is to wind the silver mylar to the hook bend and secure, followed by no more than seven turns of the red wire for the rib. You can add extra turns of the wire at the fly base to make a "red butt." The final step is to paint the fly with several coats of hard clear enamel such as Sally Hansen's Hard as Nails polish to add luster and make your Chromie more durable.

Keith Findley's huge Dragon Lake rainbow, taken on a size 14 Chromie

Fly 9: The Producer

My fishing career has taken many turns, almost all for the better, starting with cutty-hunk line and worm as a very small boy fishing the Little Campbell Creek, which ran through our farm in South Langley. I managed to purchase my first fly rod when I was 11 years old. Using cheap Army and Navy flies, I did rather well fishing Fraser Valley streams. As an adult, there was a natural progression to ocean fishing for salmon, with large spring salmon on top of the list, although bucktailing for coho was extremely exciting! My quest for big springs covered such waters as the West Coast near Bamfield, the Gordon Islands north of Port Hardy, and far north to Dundas Island near the south tip of the Alaskan Panhandle, not to mention big spring hook-ups in rivers such as the Skeena! In time, I found that salmon could be caught on flies of my own making, mostly river fishing, and to better hold salmon, single-handed fly rods eventually gave way to much longer, two-handed Spey rods! I am proud to say that I have caught all of the five West Coast salmon species fly fishing, though I admit that for every salmon landed on the fly, two or more are lost! But what has this salmon dialogue got to do with such a small trout fly as a chironomid?

I mention the above in part because, as well as catching fish, I have always enjoyed eating fresh-caught fish, especially ocean salmon. However, even hooking large fish with heavy gear is truly not as enjoyable as fly casting with light equipment. With time, my trout fishing has also changed in several ways, to releasing rather than keeping almost all fish caught, to pursuing larger rather than more numerous smaller trout, and to seeking what I feel are better table fish, namely brook trout, rather than rainbow or cutthroat trout! Yes, the last few years I have been seeking out good brook trout habitats. The reason is that I find the one brook trout I keep for eating is often better than most rainbows I catch in Okanagan and Cariboo waters, although I will add that kokanee are a close second for table fare! Now, brookies are not always ready to jump into your frying pan, so some special techniques are needed to find a good brook trout or two. These fish do like underwater obstructions, such as dead trees which are very adept at catching your fly or lure! My friend Al Kouritzin has spent the past winter researching brook trout flies and recommends the "Producer," which we will examine next. What's important here is not just that it's a good fly, in this case a chironomid, but how and where to fish it. A nearby lake we like has been formed as part of the East Kelowna Irrigation District, where the original lake was raised for water storage, with trees left uncut in flooded areas. Brook trout love these spots but fishermen trolling flies or gear risk losing everything if they venture near these drowned tree places. Our plan: anchor and fly cast chironomids near the dead trees, where we know many large brookies are hanging out! And the Producer has not only proven to be good in Turtle Lake but also in a terrific brook trout lake west of 100 Mile House.

Materials

- Hook – Scud size 10 to 14
- Body – Back 1/3 red acetate floss, front 2/3 black acetate floss
- Rib – Thin red wire
- Wing – None
- Hackle – None
- Head – Dark bead
- Gills – White Glo yarn
- Thread – Fine monofilament

Instructions

The white glo yarn for the gills is threaded inside the bead, and the easiest way to do this is to pull the yarn through the bead before sliding the bead to the hook eye. Do not worry about the length of yarn sticking past the bead, as it can be trimmed to size later. You will need to pinch the hook barb, of course, in order to slide both the bead and threaded glo yarn from the hook point to hook eye. After tightly tying down the piece of glo yarn to the hook shank, thus securing the bead in place at the hook eye, you can trim the yarn projecting past the bead at the hook eye fairly short. Next, attach a thin red wire to the hook shank and let it project 3 or 4 inches past the hook bend. Now wind red acetate floss, starting part way down the hook bend, tightly and thinly towards the bead. Next, starting about 1/3 or 1/2 of the way past the hook eye, wind black acetate floss to the bead, increasing the thickness as you proceed. A key here is to use ultra thin monofilament as your tying thread, as it will be almost invisible. The difference in constructing this chironomid is the next step. Moisten all the floss with acetone using a Q-tip and then stroke the wet floss from bead to bend to kind of blend the black and red floss together. The final step is to create a rib by winding the red wire forward to the bead and tying off. Finish the fly with a coat of clear cement, and you have created a good brook trout chironomid!

A great brook trout lake, Snag

Chapter 5:

HOW TO TIE MY FAVORITE WET FLIES

Fly 10: The Classic Doc Spratley

If I had only one fly to choose when fishing Central British Columbia waters, it would be the Doc Spratley! A black body with gold or silver ribbing is the most common Spratley, but it can be tied in a variety of body colors, with green as my next choice over black.

Although I never met Dr. Donald Spratley, who lived and worked as a dentist in Mt. Vernon, Washington, I have talked with several people who intimately knew the good doctor. Sue Perrault, the granddaughter of Dr. Spratley, told me that her grandfather often fished BC Interior lakes, Hihium (pronounced Hihume) being a favorite. Sue confirmed that Dr. Spratley invented the fly sometime in the early 1940s. It was patterned after the large chironomids found in Hihium Lake. After his retirement, with his friend Leo Whitney, the good doctor spent his summers fishing the BC Interior lakes, another favorite being Janice Lake, located off Highway 24. Doc Spratley passed away in 1968, but his legacy continues to be enjoyed by fly fishers worldwide! Another knowledgeable contact was from a keen fly fisherman, Bill Shea of Kenmore, Washington. Bill grew up in Mt. Vernon, Washington, and went to Dr. Spratley for his dental work. Bill told me that a Mrs. Dorothy Prankard tied the original fly for Dr. Spratley. This was also directly confirmed by the doctor's daughter, Betty Jo Wilkens. I am very pleased with these contacts and wish to thank Sue, Bill and Betty Jo for this helpful and interesting information!

As mentioned, the Doc Spratley can be tied in a variety of colors and materials. I prefer using invisible mending thread, but standard black or colored thread can be used. Hook sizes also cover a wide range. I have found that late-season big trout on lakes such as White and Dragon seem to prefer large sizes, as big as four or even two!

Materials

- Hook – Medium shank size 4 to 14
- Tail – Guinea fowl
- Body – Black wool/phentex/mohair/chenille etc.
- Rib – Silver or gold tinsel
- Throat Hackle – Guinea fowl
- Wing – Brown pheasant tail
- Head – Peacock herl
- Thread – Fine monofilament

Instructions

Tie in the tail with guinea, sparse and not more than 1/3 the body length. Attach the tinsel and body wool to the hook shank and half hitch at the bend. Wrap the body wool to the eye and tie off. Counter-wrap the tinsel to the eye with an even spacing and tie off. Flip the hook upside-down in your vise and tie in the guinea throat hackle no longer than the hook barb, then reset the hook in the starting position. Lay a small amount of pheasant tail along the top of the fly, slightly shorter than the end of the tail, and tie in near the eye. Take care not to let the wing spring up, as you want it to lie flat and parallel along the body. Overlay another pheasant piece to achieve a low contour wing, but not too bushy. Tie in a strand or two of peacock herl at the eye, whip finish, and you have just made one of the all-time best British Columbia trout flies!

My wife Lois at Hihium Lake; the fishing was good using a Red Spratley

Fly 11: The Hart Lake Vixen

I have enjoyed the opportunity of living in Prince George on two separate occasions. My second stay in this BC working town was during the mid-1980s. My interest in fly fishing led me to the Polar Coachmen's Club, a rather informal group who liked to get together to tie flies, swap fishing stories and, yes, to even build fly rods! At these sessions, I learned to tie some interesting northern fly patterns, including the subject fishing fly, the Hart Lake Vixen. One of our mentors was Steve Head, who claimed that patterns like the black leech needed a bit of touch-up for the darker waters found in many of the Prince George vicinity lakes.

I tie several leech patterns, most often with marabou in black, brown and deep maroon colors. However, the Hart Lake Vixen is not a marabou leech; instead, it has a black mohair or seal body, black hackle flowing wings, sparse black throat hackle and the most striking feature of this fly, a bright red calf tail! The tail, it was said by the Polar Coachman old-timers, was the difference between rainbow trout in the frying pan or only eating beans on those northern fishing trips!

The test for me came when the BC Wildlife Department announced a special two-week opening on Hart Lake, about 65 kilometers north of Prince George. The lake had been stocked with a special rainbow trout strain some two years previously and, because of the abundant feed, the trout had quickly grown to as much as four pounds! Although Hart Lake had been designated as a special senior and child lake only, it was felt that the large fish were numerous enough to withstand a general public opening that June. I just had to try it, but I found the fish very moody and uncooperative on my first trip to Hart. In short, I was skunked! I tried most of my favorite patterns to no avail, including my top four: the spratley, muddler, marabou leech and shrimp. But I had seen enough large fish rolling to be drawn back there a few days later. I decided to try the red-tailed leech on a fast sinking wet line with a very, very slow retrieve. I had a couple of touches when suddenly, a powerful fish took the fly and surged away, taking half of my backing on a deep, powerful run. After a long tussle, the fish, just a touch under four pounds, was landed with the red-tailed leech firmly in its jaw. Thus was born the name that I use for this fly, the Hart Lake Vixen! As a side note, this fly also works amazingly well at Secret Lake, near Canim Lake.

Materials

- Hook – Long shank size 6 to 10
- Tail – Red calf tail
- Body – Black mohair, seal or chenille
- Rib – None
- Throat Hackle – Black saddle (optional)
- Wing – Black hackle tied back
- Head – Optional peacock herl
- Thread- Black

Instructions

Secure your tying thread (black cotton or invisible mending thread) to the hook shank and tie in a small amount of red calf tail, allowing it to project about 1/4 inch past the hook bend. My preference is to wind fairly thin mohair, hook bend to eye, or dub in black seal hair in order to give the fly body a somewhat tousled but slim appearance. A chenille body is neater, but it does not seem to work quite as well. Then tie in about three narrow black hackle feathers near the hook eye, so that the feathers flow back in low profile no more than 1/2 inch past the hook bend. I usually find that I must tie in these feathers one at a time in order to achieve the proper lie along the back. Finally, place a turn of black hackle at the hook eye, cement, whip finish, and you are ready to try the Hart Lake Vixen! Just ask Cata Clutterham or Gordie Aucoin about the effectiveness of this fly. On a warm August day, during what normally is summer doldrums for trout, I guided these fine relatives to several good trout using the Hart Lake Vixen, on two separate trips to a small Cariboo lake near 100 Mile House called, naturally, Secret Lake!

Happy lady fishers at Secret Lake using the Hart Vixen

Fly 12: The La Bounty Leech

Dentists are not always painful! Aside from being a very good professional, my Kelowna dentist for many years, Dr. Al La Bounty, was an avid outdoorsman. We have had stimulating conversations, if you can define it that way with a mouth full of dental equipment, about many aspects of the great outdoors. Fly fishing, however, appears to be Dr. La Bounty's greatest priority, and from my perspective, how can one argue with that? The good doctor can not only cast a fly with great dexterity but he also is an accomplished fly tier. I recall one early September day when we had an appointment not in a dentist's chair but at Lundbom Lake, near Merritt. Our choice of water transport that day was belly tubes and, as fly fishermen often do, we compared notes on the best fly to use before entering the water. Al showed me a blood leech unlike anything that I had seen before that he intended to fish. It was a blend of black and red seal hair dubbed evenly along the shank of a size 8 Tiemco hook. The preparation of the blend is easy: simply place equal parts of the red and black seal hair into a small electric coffee bean grinder and switch the power on. A few seconds later, you will have the perfect mix for this fly. There is one additional trick. After tying a few flies, boil a cup of water and drop the newly tied La Bounty leeches into the hot water for a couple of minutes. When you take them out, immediately smooth the seal hair back along the hook shank by firmly pulling from the hook eye to the bend several times with your thumb and two fingers. Be very careful, though, as it is quite easy to get nicked by the hook point in this operation.

Oh yes, what happened that September day on Lundbom? Al took three nice rainbows on his blood leech and I only hooked and subsequently lost one fish using a silver muddler. It was enough to convince me to tie up several of Al's special leeches. Since that day, I have had success with the La Bounty leech not only at Lundbom, but also at Hatheume and Wasny Lakes.

Materials

- Hook – Tiemco 5262 size 8
- Tail – None (a short back flow of the body material)
- Body – Dubbed black and red seal
- Rib – None
- Throat Hackle – None
- Wing – None
- Head – Optional red bead, cobra or swannundaze
- Thread – Red

Instructions

In the fly shown, a small red bead was slid through to the hook eye. Then mix equal parts of black and red seal hair. A small portable electric coffee bean grinder is excellent for this. I recommend using invisible mending thread for this fly, but red or orange tying thread will also do. I make my own dubbing tool by removing the cotton from the end of a Q-tip swab and then I screw in a very small metal eye hook, making sure that there is enough of an opening in the eye for the tying thread to easily pass through. To start on the fly, half hitch your tying thread securely near the bend of the hook. Then make about a three-inch loop with your tying thread and half hitch to the same spot on the hook shank. Attach the eye of your dubbing tool to the loop and let it hang down from the hook. Next, take some of the blended seal hair and roll it between your fingers so it stretches out about 2 1/2 inches long and place it inside the three inch thread loop. The final step is to twist the dubbing tool until the seal hair forms a thin, long, shape (the seal hair ends will stick straight out). As the loop, which is now a tightly twisted length of seal hair, was attached at the hook bend, it is a simple matter to wind it forward around the hook shank to the hook eye and tie off. You can add a turn or two of red or orange swannundaze at the eye for the final step, if you have not used a red bead initially. Cement and whip finish. After the head cement is dry, drop the fly in a cup of boiling water, extract after a minute or two, and carefully force the seal hair ends back along the fly body as described above. You can experiment with different sizes of the La Bounty leech, but my best success has been with a medium to small size.

Lundbom Lake

Fly 13: The Skinny Muddler Minnow

My career with BC Tel took me to many interesting places. Looking back, the people that I worked with were mostly great, and I will admit the work was challenging and even fun much of the time. However, as a dedicated fly fisherman, I have always believed in the motto that a poor day's fishing will beat a good day in the office! Such was the case when one fine June day, several years ago, I took a day off from my engineering communications job in Kamloops. I threw my car-topper, oars and anchor in the back of my pickup and headed out to Leighton Lake, near Tunkwa Lake, just south of Savona about an hour's drive west of Kamloops. While living in Kamloops, a fly vest and a couple of fly rods remained behind the seat of my truck from March to November, just in case I should experience a panic desire to go fly fishing!

Although the size of the trout seemed to run bigger in Tunkwa Lake, with 3- to 7-pound fish not uncommon, it was a bit windy that day, so I opted to fish the more protected but often productive Leighton Lake nearby. There the Kamloops trout, a local strain of rainbow trout, ran about a uniform 2 pounds in size. Several anchored fly fishermen were already plying a shoal not far from shore, where I intended to fish. To my surprise and delight, I recognized the master of Kamloops trout fly fishing, Jack Shaw, laying out effortless casts from a sitting position in his flat-bottomed, snub-nosed aluminum punt. He was playing a fish hooked on a small dark chironomid when I found a spot to anchor, in good water but not too near Jack or anyone else.

It was not long before I realized that this group of fishermen knew each other from the happy kibitzing continually going on, especially during the frequent and expert playing of very lively silver-bodied rainbows! As time passed without any action on my part, I looked more closely at Jack's technique. He was using a floating line with about a 15-foot leader and a weighted, black, size 14 chironomid with a fine wire copper rib. His retrieve was so slow that it was hardly perceptible, but he was rewarded with bone-jarring strikes on every second cast! Alas, I did not have a similar fly or a floating line that day. As I searched my mind for a solution, I recalled having good success using a medium sinking wet line with a sparsely dressed muddler minnow fly at other area lakes. Many days of experimenting taught me that a thinly dressed muddler with a gold body and elk hair wings rather than deer hair seemed to work much better than the standard fully dressed muddler minnow. I switched to this fly and slowed down my wet line retrieve to the point where the fly began to hit weeds near the end of every cast. Soon the joy of seeing wildly leaping Kamloops trout dancing across the riffled water was mine as well! I kept one for the table and released three more, a testimony to the sparsely tied muddler when fished slowly near the lake bottom.

Materials

- Hook – Medium shank size 6 to 10
- Tail – Guinea hen or silver squirrel
- Body – Silver or gold tinsel
- Rib – None
- Throat Hackle – Guinea hen
- Wing – A thin blend of red squirrel and elk hair
- Head – Clipped elk hair
- Thread – Fine monofilament

Instructions

First, attach a piece of gold tinsel to the hook body and allow it to hang a few inches past the hook bend. Silver tinsel will also work well in some cases, but my standby is gold. A good and inexpensive tinsel source is to cut a piece of mylar tubing about 4 inches in length and pull out the individual strands as needed. Then tie in a small amount of silver squirrel or guinea fowl projecting about 1/4 inch past the hook bend for the tail. Wrap the tinsel from the hook bend evenly to the eye and tie off. At this point, I like to take the hook out of my vise and reattach it upside-down in order to tie in a small amount of guinea hen for the throat hackle. Put the hook right side up again to complete the wing, although I admit a rotary vise does the job much quicker. Turkey feathers are part of a conventional muddler, but I have eliminated it to thin down the wing. First, tie in a bit of red squirrel hair at the eye, taking care to let it flow back along the hook shank to about the same distance as the tail. Then a small amount of elk hair, also tied in at the eye, will finish the wing. Clip the stub ends of the elk hair at the eye to form the fly head, tie off, cement, and you have finished a fly that is one of my absolute favorites!

Leighton Lake at the campground

Fly 14: The Brown Leech

A friend had just called on April 17 to tell me that the ice was finally free on White Lake. After a long, snowy winter, the craving was strong to dip a fly in that fabulous rainbow trout lake. It wasn't until Sunday the 20th that I was free to try my luck. I had tied up several brown leeches modified from a commercial version that was rather successful in early spring of the past year on White. As luck would have it, just as we arrived at the lake, a steady rain started to come down. We waited for a time, but the urge to fish was just too strong, and even though I had forgotten to bring my rain pants, we headed out on the water. And pour it did, alternating between a steady

drizzle and violent downpours! After an hour or so, my jeans felt like I had walked through a car wash and the wind gusts began to feel oh so cold. However, just as we were talking about heading in, a heavy strike rocked my fly rod and about a 3-pound White Lake rainbow leaped wildly behind the car-topper, my brown leech embedded in its jaw. The fish fought stubbornly in the steady downpour, but when I began to think about the landing net, there was a quick flip and the trout was free. The barbless hook had either worked loose or I was not diligent in keeping a tight enough line.

We tested the merits of the brown leech again on the following Thursday, and it did not disappoint us. I had four solid strikes and again failed to land a fish, but my fishing companion, Skip Wheatley, managed to land two beauties on a similar pattern, one fish weighing a good 4 pounds, thus making this fly a definite winner!

Materials

- Hook – Long shank size 6 or 8
- Tail – Red cotton embroidery floss
- Body – Rust chenille, several turns of fine lead optional
- Wing – Deep brown marabou
- Head – Small gold bead
- Thread – Fine monofilament

Instructions

Start by crimping the hook barb in order to slide a small gold bead through to the fly head. I buy a lot of my fly tying materials in sewing shops, including the embroidery floss, glass beads and the invisible mending thread used to tie this fly. I tie some of these flies weighted, because in the first few weeks after ice-out, the fish are often deep. Therefore, wind about 8 turns of fine lead wire just behind the gold bead. The tail is next, and I double a length of embroidery material to extend about one quarter inch behind the hook bend, half hitch along the hook shank, and then I cut the extended loop so that 4 strands of the floss make up the tail. Then wind your rust chenille from the bend to the gold bead and tie off. The final step is to tie in the marabou wing, and here is where the invisible thread or fine monofilament is invaluable! I use 4 or 5 separate pieces of marabou and start by tying in the first piece about 1/4 inch from the hook bend, working in each piece of marabou until I reach the gold bead at the fly head. Each piece of marabou is cut in length to reach about 3/4 inch behind the hook bend before tying it in, i.e., you end up with a marabou back of uniform length. The invisible thread allows you to tie in each separate piece along the hook shank without much distortion to the chenille body! Cement and whip finish at the head and you have just completed a winning rainbow trout fly.

A loon swimming over one of the many White Lake shoals

Fly 15: The All-Purpose Carey

Next to the Doc Spratley, the series of Carey flies with different body colors must surely be the favorite of many fly fishermen, including myself. The Carey, or Carey Special, is attributed to Colonel Thomas Carey, a keen early 20th century fly fisherman. It is an easy fly to tie and, with a variety of body colors, it can save the day when those large feeding trout get very selective. I can recall a day, wonderful except for the scary drive down the steep access trail from the microwave site, to Firth Lake north of Prince George, when a black Carey was exactly what those light-colored rainbows wanted! Another time on Salmon Lake, just as the algae bloom was starting, a yellow Carey was the perfect answer for several spirited 2-pound-plus rainbows. And equally as good, a red Carey produced many good fish a few years ago on Opacho Lake, while a green Carey did wonders for me on Little Alberts Lake near Prince George. What I am saying is that a well-equipped fly fisherman should have several Carey flies in different sizes and body colors! The best combination for me seems to lie in thin body shaping but with soft pheasant rump feathers for the wing overlay that will pulsate well during the retrieve. Try it and you will see!

Materials

- Hook – Medium shank size 6 to 10
- Tail – Optional, brown pheasant or gray grizzly hackle

- Body – Wool, phentex, dubbed seal or chenille in a variety of colors
- Ribbing – Optional, gold or silver tinsel
- Wing – Complete wrap of pheasant rump feather to form wing and hackle
- Hackle – As above
- Head – Black thread
- Thread – Fine monofilament or black

Instructions

I tie Careys with and without tails, but let's omit the tail on this fly, as I often have success either way. The body is next, and many, many materials can be effectively used. Plain old wool is a favorite in black, brown, red, yellow, purple and green, just to name a few colors that have produced for me! I usually separate the strands in about a 4 inch piece of wool in order to make a body that is slim in appearance. With a thin wool strand, you can tie one end at the fly head, lay it back along the fly shank, cinch it down at the hook bend, and then wrap it tightly back to the hook eye, where it is tied off. At this point, attach a soft pheasant rump feather and turn it 360 degrees once or twice to create both the wing and the fly hackle. Force the pheasant feather back along the hook shank by wrapping back slightly with your tying thread as you whip finish the head. Fine monofilament, which is much thinner than regular fly tying thread, does a good job of this, but black thread is fine. Cement, and you have finished a great fly!

Firth Lake, looking east down the steep access road

Fly 16: The Dynamic Bloodworm

British Columbia Interior Lake fishing in June can be absolutely outstanding, or slow as a snail race in the rain! I have managed to catch good-sized rainbow trout during these slow periods on a fly that radically overdoes the natural size and color of chironomid bloodworms that occur in many lakes. In fact, this is a fly that seems to span the differences in trout appetites almost everywhere in my home province of British Columbia. I recall catching trout on my dynamic bloodworm in such diverse areas as Tunkwa, Nulki, Lost and Aileen Lakes—remarkably, when no other fly seemed to be working! Could it be that it is so much longer and brighter than the natural lake larvae that the trout cannot resist taking a swipe at it? I will leave it for you to decide, but I can assure you from my experience, this is truly a dynamic fishing fly!

Materials

- Hook – Medium shank size 6 to 10
- Tail – None
- Body – Underlay, red seal hair, overlay red swannundaze
- Ribbing – None
- Head – Optional turn of white ostrich herl
- Thread – Fine monofilament

Instructions

This is a very simple fly to tie, but it is important to use invisible mending thread or fine monofilament as your tying thread. The very simplest way is to wind a rich red triangular cobra or swannundaze material, hook bend to eye, and tie off! Nothing else! However, my preference is to first dub the hook body with a very thin layer of red seal hair, not to create bulk, but so that the tiny ends of the seal hair protrude between the windings of the red swannundaze that is the overlay. In other words, after the hook shank is covered with a thin layer of red seal hair, secure a piece of red cobra or swannundaze at the hook bend and wind in tight turns through to the hook eye. Remember to keep the plastic wraps snug so that the fly takes on a very slim, streamlined appearance. I then sometimes add one or two turns of white ostrich herl at the hook eye before whip finishing and cementing the head. Surprisingly, I have found a longer number six fly often works better on those slow days than a fly tied on a smaller hook, which would more accurately represent the natural bloodworm. And a very slow retrieve that allows the fly to sink near the bottom usually produces the best results for me.

Lost Lake, east of Winfield

Fly 17: The Dragonfly Nymph

Chironomids may be the best way to catch early-season trout in our western lakes, but it requires a specialized technique to productively fish a chironomid, especially when the trout are being selective. Let's have a look at a fly that will work almost any time of the year, whether on a slow troll or cast, and retrieved just above the bottom weed beds. The large dragonfly nymph is an offering that trout will often hit even when feeding or other aquatic insects. There are many ways to tie a dragonfly nymph, but the two principal ones are the clipped deer or elk hair Gomphus and the longer dubbed Darner, which we will now examine. The Darner dragonfly nymph can grow to a surprisingly large size, with three legs protruding from each side of the thorax, a long, segmented body, and very small tail section appendages, which are unlike the much longer tails of damsel fly nymphs. There is a well proven theory that big flies catch big fish, so the dragonfly nymph should definitely be one of your fly-box selections!

Materials

- Hook – Long shank size 2 to 8
- Tail – Optional short goose quill, v-shaped
- Body – Dubbed dark tan or olive-green seal hair
- Ribbing – Fine copper or gold wire
- Thorax – Brown pheasant hackle, trimmed short on top and left long for legs on the sides
- Hackle – None

- Head – Optional peacock herl
- Thread – Fine monofilament

Instructions

Attach your tying thread to the hook shank and secure a fine gold wire with some half hitches so that the wire projects past the hook bend three or four inches. Now you are ready to make a dubbing loop for the seal hair. I first roll the seal hair between my fingers into a very thin cigar shape about three inches long. I then place this hair into a similar length loop of tying thread, which is allowed to hang directly below the hook bend. The next step is important. Attach a dubbing tool (I make my own out of Q-tips with the cotton swabs cut off and a tiny opened eye hook screwed into one end, which then looks like a miniature shepherd's staff) to the bottom of the loop and twist the hair tightly without breaking the dubbing loop. It takes a lot of twisting to get the seal hair into a thin line with hair ends sticking straight out. You are then ready to wrap the seal hair dubbing loop about three quarters of the way to the hook eye. Temporarily secure it here with a half hitch and place a clothes peg on what remains of your dubbing loop so that it doesn't unravel. At this point attach a pheasant hackle feather and spiral it around the hook shank not more than two turns. Lay a second pheasant hackle feather directly on top of the hook, projecting back to the hook bend, and secure both with your tying thread. Before continuing past the pheasant feathers with the seal hair dubbing loop, I like to wind the fine gold wire through to this point to form the body segments and tie off. Carefully wrap the remainder of the dubbing loop past the pheasant feathers to the hook eye and tie off there. The final step is to trim the first pheasant hackle, top and bottom, so that it projects out the side as legs. The second pheasant feather along the back must lie tight to the body, facing back to the hook bend. Cut it about ¼ inch long to make a short shell back representing the thorax. There is a bit of a trick to wind the seal hair through the pheasant feathers, shaping them as you go, so that the legs and shell back will look realistic after trimming. A final wrap of peacock herl at the hook eye is an option, but I have found that the fly will work equally well without this head.

Will this fly work? I can recall one summer evening casting a small brown dry sedge during a prolific caddis hatch on Sheridan Lake. When the hatch came on I had switched to a dry line and left the seal hair dragonfly nymph that I was using on a wet line dangling over the edge of the boat in about ten feet of water. My success wasn't too great with the dry fly sedges, but suddenly the wet line went berserk and the rod, reel, line and all was almost yanked into the lake before I could grab it. A six-pound rainbow had decided that the dragonfly nymph in the water directly below the boat was a better meal than the hundreds of small brown caddis flies hatching everywhere! On other lakes, my best success has been fishing a dragonfly deep with a wet line. My retrieve is a series of quick pulls, followed by a brief rest. Also, in order to lessen weed pickup from the bottom, a spun and clipped dragonfly made from deer or elk hair will help to prevent fouling from weeds when fished deep.

Sheridan Lake

Fly 18: The Dependable Woolly Bugger

October is woolly bugger month in our part of the world! The great hatches of summer are over and moose are more likely to be the cause of lake disturbances. But those big rainbow trout are surging with renewed vigor as they seem hell-bent on feeding orgies prior to the long winter ice-up of the lake surfaces. Fall colors are in bloom as aspen, cottonwood, maple and birch trees display their short brilliance of gold, orange and red, making the countryside a joy to behold! While many outdoor people are thinking of hunting gear, fishing in western Canadian lakes can be the best of the year! And one of the best producing flies for this time period is the woolly bugger! It is an easy fly to tie and can be effective in a variety of colors, but my favorite is dark green and black; a must in your fly box. Try it, you will like it!

Materials

- Hook--Medium shank size 4 to 10
- Tail--Black Marabou
- Body--Dark green chenille
- Ribbing--Optional gold or silver tinsel
- Thorax--None
- Hackle--Palmered black saddle hackle
- Head--Peacock herl
- Wing--None
- Thread--Fine monofilament

Instructions

It is important to use invisible mending thread or fine monofilament for this fly, as it makes it possible to back wrap the palmered hackle without much distortion of the fly body. Start by attaching your thread to the hook shank and tie in the black marabou tail, projecting back no longer than the length of the hook. Next, secure a thin black saddle hackle tip first, so that it projects outward about 1/3 of the distance from the hook bend. Then wrap the dark green chenille from the hook bend to the hook eye, being careful not to disturb the saddle hackle as you wrap past it. Now wrap the saddle hackle forward to the hook eye, with enough space between wraps so that you can see the chenille underneath. After securing the saddle hackle, I always wind the invisible mending thread back and forth once through the palmered hackle to add strength to the fly. Finally, add two or three turns of peacock herl to form a head at the hook eye, tie off, cement and you have finished a great autumn wet fly.

We have just made a dark green woolly bugger, which is my favorite color for large fall rainbows but a close second is a woolly bugger tied with various shades of purple, favoring a reddish wine color. I have also had success catching eastern brook trout with a brown woolly bugger so experimentation is the key!

Lac Des Roches looking east at the Highway 24 viewpoint

Fly 19: The Earl Anderson Stonefly

Expert fly tier, Earl Anderson, who worked in the downtown Vancouver Woodward's sporting goods department for many years, was my first fly tying teacher. I still feel that I owe much to Earl for his patience, dedication and extraordinary expertise in all aspects of fly fishing. Having broken a kneecap while coaching minor hockey (that is another story!) and been fitted with a plaster cast for many weeks, I found the inspiration to sign up for a night school course in fly tying, a dream that had been pushed aside with the continuing excuse, "I'm too busy now and will do it next year!" The hockey accident turned out to be a lucky break as my instructor for the fly tying course turned out to be the late Earl Anderson, and I still use the fundamentals that he taught many years ago.

It is only fitting that we look at a fly that Earl invented to imitate the large stone fly nymphs that can be found in BC waters such as the Mahood River. However, the effectiveness of this fly is not restricted to rivers. It can at times perform marvelously well in such great still water places as Dragon Lake, which is a few kilometers south of Quesnel. Earl's philosophy was that big flies will catch big fish, and I have found that to be certainly true while fishing for those huge rainbows in Dragon Lake using the Earl Anderson stonefly nymph.

Materials

- Hook--Medium to long shank size 4 to 10
- Body--Yellow wool with an overlay of dark brown wool.

- Ribbing--Visible cross hatch of heavy dark tying thread
- Hackle--Palmered olive hackle 1/2 of the body, hook eye towards the bend
- Head--Peacock herl
- Thread--Black or dark brown

Instructions

The best wool for the fly body is a coarse, large size variety, almost approaching the size of some smaller yarns used by steelheaders. Start by wrapping the yellow wool hook bend to eye in a fairly loose manner and tie off. Then lay a smaller strand of rich dark brown wool along the top of the body and, starting at the hook eye, run your tying thread to the hook bend and back again, purposely creating bumps in the brown wool back. This creates a very visible cross hatch rib, a desired feature of the fly. The spacing of the tying thread wraps should be far enough apart to allow you to use a bodkin to pull out the yellow wool between the thread gaps all along the body. I now like to tie off the black thread and tie in my invisible mending thread about 1/2 of the way from the hook bend, and at this point, palmer an olive hackle forward to the hook eye. Trim off the top half of the olive hackle to create the illusion of legs. The last step is to place a few turns of peacock herl to form a head at the hook eye, whip finish, cement and you have just created a famous BC fly, the Earl Anderson Stone Nymph!

A nice Dragon Lake rainbow pending release

Fly 20: The Dependable Shrimp or Scud Fly

Fall in the Okanagan is certainly a favorite time of year. Leaves start to color in all their splendor! Birds and animals of the wild seem to take on new energy as the heat of summer passes. And, of great importance to the fly fisher, the summer doldrum period is over and trout become active feeders again! Often as not, trout are seeking shrimp or scuds, usually near weedy bottoms. The classic shrimp pattern, the Werner Shrimp, was made famous by a well-known Interior fisher, Werner Schmid. His fly features a deer hair back with a rear swept green seal body, but there are really countless variations of shrimp imitations including backs of hair, plastic, hackle feather and bodies of many different colored materials!

My friend for many years, Al Kouritzin, recently suggested that we try a new lake, new at least to me, east on a logging road off the Big White road, less than an hour from Kelowna. The lake is called Never Touch and can now be accessed on a fairly new logging road arm pushed in to harvest a timber burn near the lake. Our BC Forest Service has provided small-boat lake access in two locations, plus a few overnight and picnic camp spots. I was impressed with the layout and, although the fishing was not exceptional, I really enjoyed the overall lake setting! Besides the three very scrappy rainbows that we landed, we were rewarded with a close-up view of a cow and calf moose feeding near the water's edge! Those Never Touch rainbows preferred a light green shrimp pattern that I will call the Never Touch Scud. As soon as we tried this fly, the action changed from nonexistent to fast and furious!

Materials

- Hook – Short shank size 10 to 16
- Tail – Short extension of the olive mallard back
- Body – Build up the shank center with green phentex or wool, light green larva lace over this, and cap the body with dyed olive mallard or wood duck
- Rib – None
- Hackle – None
- Legs – Light green hackle palmered head to tail and clipped short
- Head – None
- Wing – None
- Thread – Fine monofilament

Instructions

Start by building up the center of the shank with green wool or soft phentex. Next, wrap a piece of light green larva lace, hook bend to hook eye, to form a cigar-shaped body. Now tie in a green hackle feather near the hook eye and palmer it back in gapped turns like a rib to the hook bend. The advantage of using invisible thread is now evident, as you can carefully wrap it back to the hook bend and tie off the hackle feather with little distortion. This firmly secures the hackle wrap, which is then trimmed completely off the top and just short of the hook barb on the underside to form the legs. The final step is to tie in a dyed olive mallard flank feather at the hook eye, secure it well there, then make a second tie point at the hook bend with just enough of the mallard feather projecting past to make a short tail. Tie off, cement and you have completed a Never Touch Scud pattern!

Never Touch Lake, looking southeast on a cloudy day

Fly 21: Tony's Fly

June is a favorite month for lake rainbows in our part of the world. A good friend of mine, Tony Lillington, suggested that we fish Hatheume Lake just west of Kelowna, BC, one fine June day a few years ago. At that time, the lake was strictly catch and release, although now, thanks to some prudent fisheries management, a limit of one trout may be retained for the table. With the always-present loons for added company, we launched Tony's canoe and started a cast, troll and search adventure for the Hatheume rainbows. It wasn't long before Tony's rod arched with a wild, leaping rainbow of some two pounds plus. After the second or third fish that he had released, and without a nibble on my fly, I became very interested in what Tony was using. It turned out that Tony's successful fly was a mohair leech, of dark maroon or burgundy color. Fortunately, Tony had a couple of extras and was willing to share the bounty with me! We landed and released many fish that day, mostly on Tony's dark maroon mohair leech, so I will share the very simple tying procedure with you.

Materials

- Hook – Medium shank size 6 to 12
- Tail – Burgundy or maroon mohair, which is actually part of the body
- Body – Burgundy or maroon mohair
- Ribbing – None
- Head – Optional black thread

- Thread – Thin monofilament (optional black thread for a head)

Instructions

Tony's burgundy leech is an extremely simple fly to tie. Start by attaching a 5-inch length of burgundy mohair to the hook shank and cinch it at the hook eye. Wrap it back from there to the hook bend and then forward to the hook eye. The next step is very easily accomplished with invisible mending thread. Simply fold the mohair back along the top of the hook shank and wind your thread to the hook bend and then back to the hook eye, pushing the mohair fibers so that most of them are parallel with the hook shank. Finally, trim off the remaining mohair about the length of the hook shank past the hook bend to form the tail of the fly. If a lot of the mohair fibers are still at right angles to the hook body, you can drop the fly into a cup of boiling water for a minute and then carefully press the fibers backward to give that leech-like appearance to the fly! If you wish, add a head of black floss or thick tying thread before cementing.

Tony Lillington and Jessie at Hatheume Lake

Fly 22: Joe's Fly

I have seen a lot of home-invented flies. I am also not the least surprised that many of them work, and some far better than others! A friend of mine now passed, Joe Porkolab, took up fly fishing rather late in life but, with his lovely wife Melva, attacked the sport with such a passion that he quickly made up for any lost time. Joe went for broke, purchasing good fly fishing equipment at the start, including float tubes and fly-tying supplies. The pattern that we will now examine was a fly given to me by Joe. Where he obtained this pattern I am not sure, but I can attest that the fly

does work in many BC Interior lakes, including one of my favorites, Campbell Lake, located in the Robbins Range plateau, south and east of Kamloops. Either casting from an anchored car topper with a sink tip line or slow trolling on a #2 wet line, the Campbell Lake rainbows seemed to relish Joe's fly, taking it boldly with explosive strikes! I am also happy to report that this fly can be very easily tied as follows.

Materials

- Hook – Medium shank size 8
- Tail – Deep red or orange marabou
- Body – Orange wool
- Hackle – Palmered gray grizzly hackle
- Wing – None
- Thread – Fine monofilament

Instructions

Start by tying in a marabou tail, dark red or orange. I prefer a thick tail, which can be built up by three or four layers of marabou, although I make sure that the tail is not too long, no more than 1/2 inch behind the hook bend. Then attach a long, slender grizzly hackle tip first to the hook shank and allow it to project past the hook bend. The next step is to wrap an orange wool body hook bend to hook eye, keeping it on the slender side. Now palmer the grizzly hackle from the tail to the hook eye with 5 or 6 evenly spaced wraps. Tie off, cement, and you have just completed Joe's fly. An option is to use some orange or red tying thread to form a head at the hook eye, but I have found the fly to be just as successful in Campbell Lake without the head!

Campbell Lake

Fly 23: The Skagit Fullback

When I lived in Vancouver, my two favorite fly fishing rivers were the Vedder and the Skagit. Because of the crowded conditions during the coho and steelhead winter seasons on the Vedder, a very special retreat for me during the summer months, which are generally considered off-season for fly fishers, was a trip to the upper reaches of the Skagit River. I would hike down the east side of the river from the confluence of the Sumallo and Skagit Rivers for more than a kilometer. This often found me past most of the roadside fishermen. I found sunny weather usually resulted in midday hatches and often great dry fly fishing! Consequently, I usually spent most of my time dry flying that beautiful river but a seldom failed standby fly for me was a fullback tied fly when top action ceased. When conditions were not right for surface hatches, this fly fished wet was nearly always a producer and therefore a valuable addition to your fly box!

Materials

- Hook – Long shank 2 to 3x size 2 to 10
- Tail – None
- Body – Thin black wool or black chenille overlaid with dark moose hair
- Ribbing – None
- Hackle – Brown hackle tied in palmer style
- Head – Short clipped moose hair
- Thread – Fine monofilament

Instructions

Attach a thin strand of black wool at the hook bend. Also tie in a small clump of dark moose hair tip, first along the hook shank, and allow the hair to extend past the hook bend. Then wind the wool through to the hook eye and tie off. Next, secure a brown saddle hackle at the hook eye and palmer it back to the hook bend, shaping the fibers to flow away from the hook eye as you wind it to the bend. If you use invisible mending thread as your tying thread, you can easily wind it back to the hook bend and forward to the hook eye, shaping the hackle to flow backward without distorting the shape or color of the body. The final step is to clip off the hackle fibers from the top and then fold the moose hair forward to the hook eye and tie off at that point. Trim the moose hair at the hook eye so that it forms a head about 1/8 inch long, projecting over the eye. Whip finish, cement, and you have completed the Skagit River fullback!

Skagit River east side trail crossing just above the Sumallo Junction

Fly 24: The Versatile Halfback

Some years past, shortly after we moved to Kamloops, BC, a long period of hot weather ended in late August. Fishing had been in the summer doldrums, and I felt a strong urge to try some fly casting for trout at one of the local lakes. Because Jocko Lake was very close to my new home in Kamloops, I hefted my trusty 10-foot car topper into my pickup truck and headed to the lake with my small dog Pepper for company. I noticed a few other fishermen at anchor when I arrived, so, not being too familiar with the lake, I anchored nearby but still at a respectable distance from the water that they were covering. A couple of hours went by with very little action, either for me or for the other anglers. I had changed flies several times and finally decided to try a brown halfback. Much to my surprise, a large Jocko rainbow decided that the halfback was just the medicine that he wanted! After a strong tussle, I released about a 4-pound fish, feeling that the recent warm weather may have imparted a muddy taste to the big rainbow. Soon after, I rowed in to shore as the evening shadows were beginning to fall. One of the other anglers also left the water to come and talk with me. He introduced himself as Irving Ross, a member of the Kamloops Fly Fishers. He said that he enjoyed watching me catch and release the large rainbow, and would I be interested in coming to a Kamloops Fly Club meeting? Of course, I felt honored about the invitation and soon after became a member of the Kamloops Fly Fishers! We will now look at how to tie a basic but often very productive fly, the versatile halfback. As you will guess, the halfback is related to our previous fullback fly but is usually tied with dark pheasant feather rather than hair.

Materials

- Hook – Medium or short shank size 2 to 14
- Tail – Brown goose quill
- Body – Fine peacock herl or brown ostrich
- Thorax – Two wraps of orange wool at the eye, plus an overlay of brown pheasant on top, 1/3 body to hook eye
- Hackle – Dark saddle hackle palmered hook eye to 1/3 body
- Head – Orange wool mostly covered
- Thread – Fine monofilament

Instructions

Start the fly by attaching two brown goose quills to form a very short "v" tail. Next wrap the hook shank with fine peacock herl or several strands of brown ostrich herl to create the fly body. The thorax is next, about 1/3 the length of the fly body. First make a couple of turns of orange wool at the hook eye, then, on top of the hook, place the quill end of a small piece of pheasant tail feather also at the hook eye and tie it down about one-third of the way back to the tail. Now palmer a brown or black saddle hackle, starting at this tie-down point, and wrap it to the hook eye. Clip the top of the hackle off and then pull the pheasant over and ahead to the hook eye and tie it off, cutting the excess material flush at the hook eye. Cement your final half hitches, and you have completed an excellent all-purpose nymph fly for a wide variety of trout waters. The halfback can also be made without the palmered saddle hackle by pulling the pheasant tail tips down and back under the thorax to form legs. In fact, a sister fly, the Pheasant Tail Nymph, is really a small halfback tied in this manner and constructed entirely out of pheasant.

A typical lake in the Merritt to Kamloops cattle range

Fly 25: The Caddis Crawler

The wind blew in spurts on a chilly October day at Buck Lake. The gray day hinted of snow soon to come in the Douglas Lake Ranch plateau. There were no obvious hatches in the cool weather to provide a hint of what the larger rainbow and occasional brook trout might be feeding on in the lake depths. On a hunch, I changed to a sink tip fly line and a weighted caddis crawler to search the bottom near the small west-end island. After a few casts, my line suddenly tightened with the unmistakable pull of a heavy fish. Several minutes later I was rewarded with a rainbow trout, just over two pounds, clean and silver as they come! The recipe for this excellent lake nymph is as follows.

Materials

- Hook – Long to medium shank streamer size 10
- Body – Dark olive swannundaze, small
- Thorax – Hareline dubbin, March Brown #2 (light tan)
- Hackle – Brown hen hackle feather
- Head – Olive wool, thin or optional peacock herl
- Thread – Fine monofilament

Instructions

For best success, I have found that several wraps of thin pencil lead just back of the hook eye will help to keep the fly near the bottom, where it has proven to be most effective. Next, attach and wrap your thin dark olive swannundaze, starting part way down the hook bend, and wrap up the shank over the lead near the hook eye. At this point, make a dubbing loop with your tying thread and insert a small amount of the March Brown material into the loop, twist and form a short thorax not more than 1/4 the length of the hook shank. At the thorax head near the hook eye, apply one or two turns of short brown hackle feather and clip the top. The final step is a couple of turns of dark olive wool or peacock herl for the head, taking care to push the hackle back to the hook point as you complete the head. Cement, tie off, and you have finished my caddis crawler.

Buck Lake, photographed at the BC Forest Campsite

Fly 26: Bill's Brown Bomber

Bill Shea of Kenmore, Washington, was an avid fly fisherman all his life. He grew up in Mt. Vernon, Washington, where Dr. Donald Spratley was his dentist. Bill first contacted me when he read my Internet article on the famous Doc Spratley fly. I have since learned much from Bill, not only with regard to details about Dr. Spratley, but also about the many fly patterns that Bill himself has tied. From my inspection of many of his flies, it was evident that Bill was an expert fly maker in his own right. So we will examine one of his favorite self-invented flies. Sadly, my friend passed away after a short illness on May 30, 2013, so the fly fishing and tying world has indeed lost a great champion!

Materials

- Hook – Medium shank size 4 to 8
- Tail – Brown marabou
- Body – Brown chenille
- Ribbing – None
- Hackle – Brown hen hackle palmered from the hook bend to the bead
- Head – Clear or silver bead
- Wing – None
- Thread – Fine monofilament

Instructions

Start by crimping your hook barb so that you can slide a silver or clear glass bead through to the hook eye. Next, secure a clump of brown marabou to the hook shank to form a tail equal to the length of the body. Bill favors a brown for both the tail and body that is more of a rust shade than either light or dark brown. Next, select a long brown hen hackle with short fibers and tie in tip first at the hook bend. Then attach a piece of medium-sized rust brown chenille to the hook shank and wind forward to the bead at the hook eye. The final step is to palmer the brown hackle from the hook bend to the bead at the hook eye and tie off at that point, cement, and you have completed Bill's Brown Bomber. Bill recommends using his fly on those slow fish days. He also advises to keep the retrieve low and slow, with short pulls!

Bill Shea on an eastern Washington State lake

Fly 27: The Near Classic Egg and I

Late April can be the start of a magical time on Shuswap Lake. Salmon fry, some years in their millions, begin the long and dangerous trek to the Pacific Ocean. Here is where the classic "Egg and I" fly can come into its own. Large, marauding rainbow trout love to feed on the racing fry and will sometimes strike a well-placed "Egg and I" fly. The Classic fly is tied with a grey tail and silver body, but I have found equal success using a yellowish tail and a hint of blue in the body. It certainly won't hurt to have both versions in your fly box, so we will have a look at how I tie my "Egg and I" fly.

Materials

- Hook—Medium to long shank size 2 to 8
- Tail – Yellow wood duck
- Body – Underlay blue tinsel, overlay silver clear flashabou, front gold tinsel
- Hackle – Radiant red yarn or chenille as a throat hackle
- Head – Red tying thread
- Wing – Mallard flank feather, optional overlay a few strands of clear crystal hair
- Thread—Fine monofilament and change to red for the head

Instructions

Start with a short yellow or gold-dyed wood duck feather for the tail. Next, form the body in three stages, beginning with a wrap of blue tinsel. Overwrap this with clear flashabou, allowing the blue to show underneath. The third step is to make just a few wraps of gold or copper tinsel near the hook eye, so that only a tiny amount is visible in the finished fly. Now tie in a short piece of radiant red yarn or chenille for a short throat hackle. Add a mallard flank feather wing with a flat profile, flowing back just past the tail. You can then add a few strands of clear flashabou or crystal flash as an option. The final step is to create a neat head. I prefer red tying thread, although the classic "Egg and I" usually features a black head. By the way, you should have several of these flies, because if you find a place where those giant rainbows are actively feeding, you will likely need more than one fly!

Trolling on Shuswap Lake; Copper Island distant left

Fly 28: The Bead Head

A few years ago I made a delightful trip to Nimpo Lake in the Chilcotin country of west-central British Columbia as a guest of Richard and Colleen Haavik. Rich and Colleen operated a fishing lodge called Rainbow Resort, mainly catering to American customers, flying them in to a host of area lakes and rivers for some of the best fly fishing experiences imaginable! When I arrived, the last of their summer guests had departed, so Rich treated me to one of his favorite fly fishing stretches for rainbow trout on the upper Dean River. We caught trout after trout on dry flies and then, for a change of pace, Rich gave me a bead head fly and demonstrated how to fish it using a strike indicator about half way up the leader. Immediately we were into fish, many of which were larger than the fish attacking our dry flies a few minutes earlier. Let's have a look at Rich's bead head fly, which is so effective on the Dean River.

Materials

- Hook—Short shank size 10
- Tail – Short black squirrel
- Body – Black seal
- Rib – Fine copper wire
- Thorax – Thicker black seal overlapped with a few strands of black goose feather
- Hackle – None
- Head – Gold bead
- Thread – Fine monofilament

Instructions

Crimp the hook barb and slide the gold bead to the hook eye. A couple of wraps of lead wire just behind the bead will ensure that the fly will quickly sink in faster water. Next, tie in a short tail of black squirrel. Attach a piece of thin copper wire to the hook shank and let it project past the tail. Now form a dubbing loop of black seal hair, winding it forward thinly from the hook bend and thicker from about the center of the hook shank to the bead at the hook eye. However, before completing the thicker half, attach a few strands of goose quills at the center of the hook shank and then wind the copper wire forward to form a rib along the thin half of the body. After completing the thicker thorax as mentioned earlier, the final step is to fold the goose quills forward to the bead and tie off at that point. Cement, and you have finished an excellent Dean River wet fly!

Rich Haavik and a wild Dean River rainbow

Fly 29: The Idaho Nymph

The Idaho Nymph has long been one of my favorite flies. A fly fisher friend first introduced me to this fly when he achieved great success fishing Watch Lake, just above Green Lake in the Central Cariboo. The surprising fact was that it was mid-summer, a time when trout fishing is usually deemed to be in the doldrums and golf is the better activity! He was camped at Watch Lake and observed that fish were surface rolling as evening approached. He recounted that he tried several flies but only had success when he used an Idaho Nymph, fished just under the surface. I have also experienced great success with this, fly fishing it at our Canim Lake summer camp and also at a small, picturesque walk-in lake near Kelowna, Walker Lake.

Materials

- Hook – Mustad 9672 size 8 to 12 or Eagle Claw L1197N silver
- Tail – Black saddle hackle
- Body – Black chenille, phentex, yarn or wool
- Ribbing – Black ostrich herl
- Thorax or wing case – White goose quill
- Hackle – Black saddle palmered through the front third of the body
- Head – Optional peacock herl
- Wing – None
- Thread – Thin monofilament

Instructions

Select a small amount of black saddle fibers and tie in a tail no longer than one-third of the hook length. Next attach a piece of black wool (chenille, phentex, etc.) and also a black ostrich herl to the hook shank. First, wind the wool hook bend to the hook eye, then counter wrap the ostrich herl as an evenly spaced rib to the hook eye. Then tie in a thin black hackle, tip first, plus a piece of white goose quill on top of the hook and cinch down the hook eye to a point about a third of the shank distance from the eye. Wind the hackle forward to the hook eye and tie off. Trim the top hackle, then fold the white goose quill forward to the hook eye and also tie off. The final step is to make a head with a few turns of peacock herl at the hook eye. Cement, and you have finished the Idaho Nymph!

Walker Lake, a small pretty walk-in gem

Fly 30: The Vinson Emerger

A trap shooter acquaintance, Mark Gilbert, has taken many large trout from Vinson Lake, which is located in the high country several kilometers south on the Buck Lake logging road south off the Okanagan Connector. His favorite method is to wait for a late evening sedge hatch to connect with the large cruising rainbows using a dry fly. On more than one occasion, before the sedges started rising in earnest, Mark noticed another fly fisherman hitting fish after fish just under the surface! Of course, curiosity soon moved Mark to ask, "What are you using?" The successful fisherman did share his secret, and Mark has been good enough to allow me to pass on this information to you! The fly was a small emerger fished slowly just under the surface; a fly that the very large Vinson rainbows gulped with wild abandon! It is also surprisingly easy to tie, as follows.

Materials

- Hook – Mustad 3399A size 10
- Tail – None
- Body – Dark green or brown chenille
- Ribbing – Fine silver wire
- Thorax – None
- Hackle – Short blue pheasant rump feather
- Head – Black tying thread
- Wing – None
- Thread – Black

Instructions

Attach both the dark chenille and fine silver wire at the hook bend. Wind the chenille to the hook eye and tie off. Follow this with about five turns of the wire, also to the hook eye. Next, create a beard hackle using a short blue pheasant feather with the tips extending back to the hook barb. Complete this very simple but effective fly by forming a head with your black tying thread. Cement, tie off, and you have finished an excellent Vinson Lake Emerger fly!

Vinson Lake, looking southeast

Fly 31: The Skinny Minny

During my career with the telephone company, I was transferred several times throughout the grand province of British Columbia. I must say that the two years I spent in Kamloops were an absolute delight from a fly fisherman's point of view! I learned much about the finer points of the sport from several expert fly fishermen whom I had the good fortune to meet during my time in Kamloops. My neighbor across the street, John Wright, was such a person. He seemed to enjoy my endless questions about tying flies, especially those that worked in the area lakes and also how best to present them at different times of the year. A fly that John showed to me was his Skinny Minny, very effective if fished properly with a very slow retrieve. It is well worth having a close look at John's fly!

Materials

- Hook – Medium to short shank size 6 to 10
- Tail – Brown pheasant rump feather
- Body – Thin brown pheasant rump feather ribbed with brown tying thread
- Ribbing – Brown thread (Optional black)
- Hackle – Brown pheasant
- Head – Brown tying thread
- Thread – Brown (Optional black)

Instructions

As the name implies, this fly is tied extremely thin! Start by placing the hook barb side up in your vise. Lay a small amount of brown pheasant rump feather along the underside of the shank, with the tips projecting 1/4 inch past the hook eye. Snug the pheasant tightly along the shank with your tying thread and then fold the feather tips back to make a thin throat hackle. Flip the hook right-side-up in your vise, and now lay another thin clump of pheasant rump feather along the top of the shank, this time allowing the tips to project 1/4 inch past the hook bend to form the tail. Rib this with your tying thread to make the back appear segmented. As you tie off at the hook eye, take care to keep the throat hackle in place. Cement, and you have finished John Wright's very productive Skinny Minny fly. He advises to fish this fly with a very slow retrieve, chironomid style!

Casey, Pepper and Allen, on a north Kamloops area lake

Fly 32: The Oyama Lake Special

One day a few years ago, my friend Joe Porkolab returned from Oyama Lake in the plateau country just east of Winfield, BC, with stories of terrific rainbow trout fishing. He went on to say that one particular fly was simply dynamite for attracting fish in that lake of many small islands. I insisted on having a look at the fly and was somewhat surprised to see that it was an attractor pattern, not closely resembling the insect population of Oyama Lake. However, I would certainly not argue with Joe's success and would like to share the details of the fly that worked so well for Joe and his friends!

Materials

- Hook – Medium shank size 6 to 8
- Tail – Red wool or calf tail
- Body – Brown floss
- Rib – Gold tinsel
- Wing – Green wood duck
- Throat – Brown hackle tied full
- Thread—Fine monofilament

Instructions

Start by tying in a short piece of red wool for the tail. Next secure a length of gold tinsel at the hook bend followed by the brown floss which is wrapped hook bend to hook eye to create a smooth but thin body. Over this, wind the gold tinsel in 6 or 7 even turns to the hook eye. Now attach the green wood duck wing near the hook eye, allowing the wing to flow back over the body to about the end of the tail. The final step is to wind a few turns of brown hackle at the head, tie off, cement and you have finished an excellent attractor pattern, the Oyama Lake Special!

I was very pleased to receive an email from Alan K. Spiller of St. Albert, Alberta, who provided an interesting history of the Oyama Lake Special. Allow me to share it with you. Alan's late father, Cec Spiller, was born in Penticton, BC. Although he was a 60-year Alberta resident, he came west to fish Oyama Lake faithfully for many years. During Cec's annual trips to Oyama, he continually experimented with various flies. Cec finally found the best success with an attractor fly of his own creation, the Oyama Lake Special! Alan has confirmed that this fly is a terrific producer on Oyama Lake and also has caught fish on many other lakes.

Oyama Lake, photographed at the BC Forest Campsite

Fly 33: The Driemel Fly

Without a doubt, Barry Driemel is one of the best long-distance (handicap) trap shooters in British Columbia. Some years ago, I met Barry at one of the Vancouver Island shoots, which he frequently attended when he and his wife, Ruth, resided near Port Albernie. In those days, Barry was a regular steelhead and salmon fisher on those great Vancouver Island rivers such as the Somass and the Stamp. A few years past, Barry and Ruth moved to the Armstrong area, where he has continued his excellent trap shooting at the North Okanagan Trap and Skeet Club. And in my view, quite important, he also does some trout fishing when time permits.

Since we are both members of the same shooting club, I see Barry fairly often. Not long ago, Barry showed me the remnants of a fly that he had great success with at Nimpo Lake in the Chilcotin. Those large, slashing rainbows literally chewed the fly to pieces, so Barry, knowing that I was a fly tier, asked if I could reconstruct it and perhaps tie him a few more. "Certainly," I said, "if I can see it, I can tie it!" In no time I rebuilt the original and also made several more copies for Barry. I really like the look of this fly and wish to share this pattern with you! Let's call it the Driemel fly.

Materials

- Hook – Eagle Claw L1197N size 6
- Tail – Extra soft black craft fur with a few strands of green crystal flash

- Body – Medium peacock crystal chenille
- Hackle – Black saddle palmered throughout the body
- Head – Large orange ceramic bead
- Thread - Fine monofilament

Instructions

First, crimp the hook barb and slide a large orange glass or ceramic bead to the hook eye. Follow this with a clump of soft black craft fur for the tail and clip fairly short. Mix in a few strands of green crystal flash the same length as the tail. Next, attach a piece of medium green or peacock crystal chenille to the hook shank. Wind the chenille forward, hook bend to the bead at the hook eye, and tie off. The final step is to select a long, black, thin saddle hackle and half hitch it just behind the orange bead. Wind one turn here, then carefully wind the feather back with about 1/8 inch gaps to the hook bend at the tail. The advantage of using invisible thread comes into play here, as now you can back wrap the thread through the palmered hackle to the tail without distorting or changing the appearance of the fly body. Make a couple of very tight turns of the fine monofilament at the tail, and then carefully wrap the thread forward to the hook bead and tie off there. This ensures that the hackle will not easily come apart when fish strike at the fly! A dab of cement here will finish the fly. I think it is a winner, so good luck with the Driemel Fly! Just the other day Barry informed me that during the first week of June 2016, he used this fly on Sheridan Lake and couldn't keep off numerous three- and four-pound rainbows!

Nimpo Lake, taken at Rainbow Lodge on the west shore

Fly 34: The Knouff Lake Special

Knouff Lake is a pretty lake lying about an hour's drive into the ranching country north and a little east of Kamloops, BC. It was one of the many barren lakes in the Kamloops plateau country around the turn of the 20th century, without fish, but loaded with aquatic insects, especially large traveling sedges. In the spring of 1917, local ranchers decided to release a few spawning rainbow trout captured from a Paul Lake stream. This rather innocuous act was not forgotten, and exactly three years later, a group of fly fishermen descended on the lake, not really knowing what to expect. The fishing they experienced was beyond their wildest imagination, as many large trout were landed that day, the biggest weighing in at an astonishing 17 pounds! Knouff Lake soon became known as a fishermen's paradise for catching large rainbows on a dry fly, thanks to the proliferation of those huge traveling sedges. A wet fly was also developed to imitate the sedge pupa during periods when the sedges were not hatching. It was called the Knouff Lake Special, well worth a look!

Materials

- Hook – Medium shank size 4 to 10
- Tail – Golden pheasant neck feather barbs
- Body – Red or green Uni-mylar
- Ribbing – Peacock herl
- Thorax – None
- Hackle – Brown saddle

- Head – None
- Wing – Blue pheasant rump feather
- Thread—Fine monofilament

Instructions

Tie in a few barbs of golden pheasant neck feather (the kind with banded tips) on the hook shank to form a tail. Next, secure a long peacock herl and also a piece of Uni-mylar (the product that is green on one side and red on the other) to the hook shank near the bend so that they project well past the tail. Then wind the Uni-mylar forward to the hook eye, either red or green showing, depending on which way you wind the strip. This is followed by a ribbing of peacock herl, hook bend to hook eye. At this point I like to wind my invisible thread back to the hook bend and forward again to the hook eye so that the peacock herl won't be ripped off at the first slash of a big trout! This is one of the distinct advantages of using fine monofilament, as the back wind does not affect the appearance of the fly too much but does make it much stronger. Of course, a reverse technique can also be applied by making a body of solid peacock herl and using the Uni-mylar as the ribbing. You now place a blue pheasant rump feather at the hook eye and tie down so that it flows back over the body about as long as the end of the tail. The final step is to wind a turn or two of brown saddle hackle at the hook eye, cement, tie off, and you have finished a version of the famous Knouff Lake Special.

Badger Lake, next to Knouff Lake

Fly 35: The Nicomekl

As a boy, my home streams were the Little Campbell and the Nicomekl River. The Little Campbell ran through our property, a smaller stream than the Nicomekl and also much swampier, with brush-laced beaver channels, making fly fishing quite a challenge! The "Nic," as termed by my fishing friends, was in its very early years, contoured by dikes in much of its Langley to Mud Bay flow, undoubtedly limiting its fish-producing potential. However, it still managed to give up trout, steelhead and coho salmon in season to determined fishermen. It was also a great place to practice one's fly casting, as long stretches of treeless dikes allowed almost unimpeded casting! I recall spending many hours doing just this, especially when coho salmon were running in late October and November. In those days, I did not tie my own flies, depending instead on buying one or two from Bishop's Sports store in Langley when I could afford it, or on very rare occasions, a trip to the Army and Navy store in New Westminster netted perhaps a dozen flies at bargain prices!

A favorite fly at that time was the appropriately named "Nicomekl." I cannot remember where I obtained this fly, but I do recall the strong pull of a coho salmon as it fought my fly in its home river. I was devastated when the salmon broke my leader and disappeared with the fly, the only one that I owned! I can smile today at my long-ago predicament, and perhaps there is a silver lining to my loss as I can now share the fly dressing with you.

Materials

- Hook – Medium shank size 4 to 8
- Tail – Golden pheasant tippets
- Body – Back half orange wool and front half burgundy chenille or wool
- Ribbing – Gold wire (original orange tinsel)
- Hackle – Burgundy beard
- Head – None (optional black thread or peacock herl)
- Wing – Brown mallard flank tied low
- Thread – Fine monofilament

Instructions

Tie in the golden pheasant tail first, then add the gold wire and a thin strip of orange wool to the hook shank. Wind the wool forward until it covers half of the hook shank where you will tie in a piece of burgundy chenille or wool. Now wind the burgundy material forward to the hook eye and tie off. Then wind the gold wire through to the hook eye in 6 or 7 turns to form a rib. A burgundy hackle is the next step, either by making a few turns of your feather at the hook eye and trimming the top or by pinching the material to form a throat hackle. Add a low brown mallard or wood duck wing, tie off, cement, and you have finished the Nicomekl wet fly!

The Nicomekl River, downstream from 168 Street in Surrey

Fly 36: Nation's Silvertip Sedge

A recent look at one of my fly boxes tied many years ago revealed several Bill Nation patterns that I used with a reasonable degree of success when I lived in Kamloops. Bill Nation was born in England on June 29, 1881, but spent most of his life as a fishing guide in the Kamloops area, first on Shuswap's Little River. Then he established a base at Echo Lodge on Paul Lake. In those early years, large Kamloops trout could be found in many Kamloops lakes, and Bill Nation was well known for meeting client expectations. He would advertise at least 100 trout per week, with up to 60 pounds of trout per day, all on the fly! Bill Nation passed away in the fall of 1940, but he is still remembered for his many original fly patterns that he used when guiding his clients to those amazing catches.

Nation's fly patterns for the most part are not exact replicas of naturals, perhaps because Bill did not have access to the fly tying materials that we have now. However, though many of his patterns are gaudy and bright, catch fish they did, and they continue to do so to this day! I think it is quite fitting to honor this early British Columbia fly fishing pioneer by reviewing one of his fly patterns, the Silvertip Sedge.

Materials

- Hook – Medium shank size 6 to 12
- Tail – Red goose strip

- Body – Back third silver tinsel and then green seal or wool to the eye
- Ribbing – Silver oval tinsel
- Hackle – Badger
- Wing – Mallard flank tied low
- Thread – Fine monofilament (Bill's originals were tied with black silk)

Instructions

Tie in the red goose strip tail, then continue with a piece of flat silver tinsel and a second oval tinsel cinched at the hook bend. Wind the flat tinsel forward to about a third of the hook shank and complete the body to the hook eye with either dubbed green seal or green wool. Now wind the oval tinsel in 6 or 7 turns to the hook eye to form the rib. Next, wrap about two turns of badger for the hackle at the hook eye, followed by a mallard wing on top, tied low against the fly body. Cement, tie off, and you have completed Nation's Silvertip Sedge! Note: I have also seen this pattern tied with both brown mallard flank and brown turkey as the wing material.

Paul Lake, looking southeast from the BC Provincial campsite

Fly 37: The Bright Damsel

Several years ago, I took my boys and a couple of visiting nephews from Edmonton to Hyas Lake, just an hour or so north-east of Kamloops. It was a fine June day, a warm sun filtering through the newly leafed trees and just the right amount of wind to put a gentle ripple on the water. A few sedges were emerging, so I switched to a dry fly with some success, while the boys were happy to troll wet flies in the hope of getting a big one! While casting the dry fly from an anchored position, I noticed bulging just under the surface near the shore reeds, enough so that I pulled anchor to investigate. What I saw was very bright green damsel nymphs wiggling to the reeds, where they would crawl out of the water to shed their nymph casing. After drying out, they would then take off as an acrobatic damsel fly! Close observation revealed a very pronounced "wiggle" as they slowly swam and, surprisingly, a very light and bright green color!

After observing the Hyas Lake damsels, I put some thought into how I would tie a good imitation of the swimming nymph. It had to have good movement, so a soft marabou tail would help. Also, the bright green color (not blue or brown) was a surprise, so I added a wide flashabou strip on the top of the body, plus eyes that are a bit exaggerated in size, but, what the heck, it has worked just great for me!

Materials

- Hook – Medium shank size 6 to 10
- Tail – Bright green marabou

- Body – Twisted green marabou, as in the tail, with an overlay of wide fluorescent flashabou
- Rib – Soft green saddle hackle to imitate legs
- Hackle – As above
- Head – Large green eyes
- Wing – None
- Thread - Fine monofilament

Instructions

Start by tying in a light, bright green marabou tail. I often use the same marabou to wrap a fairly thin body next, although you can also make the body using chenille if you have the same color. Prior to the body wrap, I tie in a soft, light green saddle hackle tip first, just ahead of the tail. After you finish the body, add a wide, flat strip of fluorescent flashabou on top and, using invisible thread as your tying material, you can secure it well without affecting body color! I now add a set of home-constructed eyes. I buy multicolor beads at a craft store and I string two green beads on a piece of heavy nylon fishing line. You can make a tiny barbell with the beads with a butane torch to secure the beads no more than 1/8 inch apart by burning the nylon (on the outside) snugly against the beads. Next, figure-eight the nylon eyes with your tying thread just behind the hook eye. The last step is to wrap the saddle hackle hook bend to the eyes as a spaced rib, to create the impression of legs by trimming off the top. Tie off, cement, and you have finished an irresistible trout fly!

Son Trevor fishing Hyas Lake

Fly 38: Al's Lumby Fly

I have done a lot of fishing over the years with my friend from UBC days, Al Kouritzin. As well, we have chased deer all over the Okanagan. And while Al's Brittany spaniel and my yellow Labrador retriever were alive, we spent twelve seasons hunting pheasants in Alberta! The latter activity ensured a good supply of fly tying feathers, but the real joy of those outings was watching our dogs enthusiastically work the pheasant cover! However, I digress from our fly tying subject, which is a fly borrowed from Al's collection.

Recently, Al and I made a trip to a small lake near Lumby where we have enjoyed considerable success in the past. We often load two car-top boats in the bed of our pickup truck; in this case we took my 4x4 pickup. This allows us to individually vary our fishing method, such as chironomiding, casting wet or dry flies from an anchored boat, or trolling. The action on this day was not furious, but we did enjoy several hits, mainly on trolled flies. I released three small rainbows and Al did much better when he switched to an olive-green fly that we will now examine.

Materials

- Hook – Medium shank size 8
- Tail – Olive wood duck, optional olive marabou
- Body – Olive chenille
- Rib – Both red and black thread
- Hackle – Brown rooster cape

- Head – Several turns of the red thread
- Collar – A few turns of peacock herl
- Thread – Fine monofilament

Instructions

Start by tying in a tail of olive wood duck feather. Al also uses olive marabou for the tail. Next, secure both red and black lengths of rod tying thread just ahead of the tail. Now wrap a piece of thin olive chenille from the tail to just short of the hook eye. Form the rib next by carefully making spaced turns of both the red and black thread, tail to hook eye, trying to show both colors as you make the wraps for the rib. At the hook eye, before tying off the red thread, make several turns to give a hint of red at that point. Now select a brown rooster feather with short fibers and make two or three turns a little back of the hook eye. Trim the top hackles off so just the sides and bottom part of the hackle is left. The final step is to make a thin collar of peacock herl near the hook eye but still allow the red thread wraps to show between the collar and the hook eye. Cement, tie off, and you have finished Al's Lumby fly!

A small Lumby area lake

Fly 39: The Bluey Lake Special

My friend Al Kouritzin and I recently loaded two car toppers into my truck and, with great spirits, headed out over the Connector to Courtenay Lake on a midweek day. The weather had turned reasonably warm, but the wind was blustery, with a few threatening clouds. I wanted to try Courtenay because I had noticed quite a number of fishermen working the lake on a previous Easter weekend trip to the Coast. True enough, there were no less than a dozen boats on the lake, counting ours, but few fish were being caught, at least that we could see. I managed to release one very small trout taken on a chironomid and Al did not have a touch. After a few fruitless hours, we decided to do a bit of exploring. We first drove into Lundbom, passing Marquart Lake on the way in. As usual, there were several campers spread among the shoreline trees, and the attendant revealed that a few fish were being caught, although the action was slow. Al then suggested we have a look at another vicinity lake that his neighbor, Randy, had said was good.

Bluey Lake lies south of Alleyne and Kentucky and can be reached either off the Connector's Loon road or south past Aspen Grove, where there is a turn-off left from the road to Princeton. We took the latter route as it was closer, and with some help from park attendants, we found the narrow gravel road south to Bluey Lake. By the time we arrived, it was too late for other than a quick try, but we did see an excellent, bright 20-inch rainbow landed by another fisherman that we met at the lake. I am always extremely curious in such situations about what the fish were taking, so I asked if I could see the successful fly. "No problem," was the quick reply, and that was my first look at what he said was the Bluey Lake Special. You can bet I tied up a few when I got home! Since there isn't much argument when a fly can catch 20-inch rainbows, I will share the pattern as follows with you!

Materials

- Hook – Medium shank such as a Mustad 9671 size 8 to 10
- Tail – Yellow wood duck or brown mallard
- Body – Medium brown crystal chenille
- Wing – Underlay brown crystal flash, overlay pheasant tail
- Head – 5/32 or 1/8 inch black bead
- Thread – Fine monofilament

Instructions

Crimp the hook barb and slide a black bead through to the hook eye. Next, attach a short tail of dyed yellow wood duck or brown mallard. Next, wrap the medium brown crystal chenille back and forth along the hook shank to form the fly body. Then, just behind the bead, tie in several strands of brown crystal flash. I like to take several strands and loop them back and forth, then cut the end loops after. Finish the fly with an overlay wing of brown pheasant tail. To keep the material from flaring up, I fold back and tie down the cut end, which forms a slight hump behind the bead. Trim this short and you have finished the Bluey Lake Special! The successful fisherman did say that the brown theme was important.

Bluey Lake

Fly 40: The Young Leech

It was already mid-November with only a hint of snow in the high country west of Big White in East Kelowna. The whitetail deer rut should have been in full swing, but there wasn't enough snow for tracking, so I called my friend, Al Kouritzin, to postpone a planned deer hunt from Tuesday of that week to Friday. I just had seen a picture of Kirsten Young holding a 13.5-pound rainbow trout in the Nov/Dec 2008 issue of *BC Outdoors Sport Fishing*, and you can bet this was in the back of my mind! I have fished the lake where Kirsten caught this whopper several times before, as it is little more than an hour's drive over the Connector west of Kelowna. Now, the Connector can be very treacherous and should be avoided if possible in winter conditions, but I had just heard a forecast of clear conditions on the highway. Since the weather was too warm for deer hunting, why not make a late season trip to this lake of giant trout?

Therefore, on a bit of an impulse, I threw my car topper into the back of my truck, along with my fly fishing equipment, and headed west to Kirsten's lake. When I arrived, there was only one other vehicle in the vicinity of the boat launch site. I quickly packed my boat and gear to the water, but before launching, I decided to walk over to a nearby couple I had noticed were busy preparing to do some fly casting from shore. Although I had never met these folks, conversation comes easy to like-minded fly fishers! They introduced themselves as Bob and Kirsten Young from nearby Merritt. "Yes," said Kirsten, "there are still some big fish in this lake, better than ever, since the stocking of triploids in several Merritt lakes, including this one. Hold on," she added, "I have a picture of a big trout I caught on a purple leech this summer!" When I saw the photo, I immediately recognized it as the one I was recently admiring in my *Sport Fishing* magazine, so I said, "Wow, I was just looking at your fish last evening!" Kirsten knew the picture of her huge rainbow had been submitted to *BC Outdoors* but they had not received a copy of the magazine, so the Youngs were very pleased that it had been published. We went on to talk about other large fish, including Bob's 8-plus-pound fish, but of even greater interest to me was that both of these grand fish were caught on a reddish maroon leech. Never wanting to miss an opportunity for more knowledge, I asked Bob if I could see a copy of this fly and he was happy to oblige! Now it's my turn to share it with you, and to credit Bob and Kirsten, we will call it the "Young Leech"!

Materials

- Hook – Medium to long shank size 6 to 8
- Tail – None, just wing flow back
- Body – Maroon sparkle antron
- Rib – None
- Hackle – None
- Head – Gold bead
- Wing – Four strands of flashabou overlaid with maroon marabou and maroon saddle hackle
- Thread – Fine monofilament

Instructions

Start by crimping the hook barb so that you can slide a gold bead through to the hook eye. Next, dub a thin body of maroon sparkle antron. If you do not have this material, a blend of equal parts of black and red seal mixed in a coffee grinder will do nicely! Now, just behind the bead, tie in three or four strands of flashabou. I like to mix silver and gold strands. A long, flat wing is next, first with thin maroon marabou, then overlaid with a maroon saddle hackle, tied low over the body and projecting well past the hook bend. Whip finish, cement, and you have completed the Young Leech, a dynamite fly for those big Merritt area hybrids!

Son Trevor and grandkids Erik and Calla at Lundbom Lake

Fly 41: Dale's Mallard Concord

For some 25 years I have prepared a monthly fly-tying article for posting on the Internet. My late wife Lois often asked me why I did all the work of preparing a fly-tying article every month when there was no compensation involved — in other words, it has always been a voluntary effort. As well, I never sell flies, but I have given away hundreds over the years! An answer to my wife's concern arrived in the mail just before Christmas. A fly tier from Prince George, Dale Ruth, sent me five of his very special flies, together with a letter explaining that he appreciated my fly-tying articles. To me, only one word can describe Dale's thoughtfulness: *priceless*! To my dear wife, I explained that was the reason I share my fly-tying recipes each month and dutifully submit to all of the preparation work involved!

Now, I have lived in Prince George on two separate occasions and have fished most of the area lakes that Dale tells me he frequently fishes. The pattern he has developed works extremely well in these lakes, and I have already proven that his fly will produce in the Okanagan and Cariboo lakes that I now fish.

Materials

- Hook – Eagle Claw 52M size 8 to 12
- Tail – None (part of overlapped wing)
- Body – Bright white floss
- Hackle – None
- Head – Small white or silver bead

- Wing – Layered brown mallard or wood duck
- Thread – Bright white 6/0

Instructions

Dale tells me that his fly is simple to tie. First, prepare at least a dozen small sized, well-proportioned mallard flank feathers, all stripped of their after feathers so that you have enough stem length, 1/2 inch or more, to easily grab. Then crimp the hook barb and slide the bead through to the hook eye. Wrap your tying thread from the bead along the shank to within 1/8 inch of the hook bend. Lightly cement the thread along the entire shank to ensure it remains secure on the shank, and then wait for the cement to dry before proceeding further.

Now take the smallest feather first and place its stem directly on top of the shank. Wrap the stem to the shank, with just a few semi-tight wraps initially. Grab the stem and pull it slowly towards the hook eye until the feather starts to close in on itself as it is being pulled under the wraps. Stop when the feather extends approximately 1/4 inch beyond the hook bend. Now lock the stem in on the shank with a few tight wraps. Excess stem can be snipped later. Next, place a slightly bigger feather on top of the first feather and complete the same procedure as before. Gradually you will work your way closer to the bead with each consecutive feather. Snip the stems close to the bead if they become too crowded (usually after the fifth feather or so). Tightly wrap them along the shank up to the bead and then back to the last feather. It is important to maintain good alignment and balance, with each feather placed on top of the shank and to each other. Within 1/8 inch or so from the bead, uniformly wrap the remaining snipped stems. Whip finish, cement, and you have completed Dale's Mallard Concord!

Dale playing a trout hooked on a Mallard Concorde at McLeod Lake

Fly 42: Fred's Deer Hair Fly

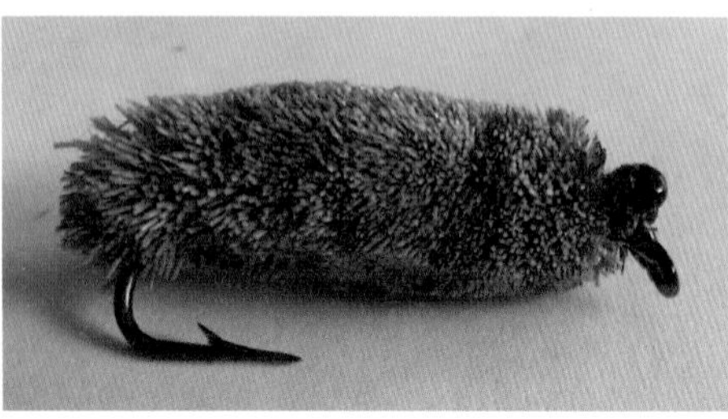

Fred McCrae is a perennial high-place finisher in the annual Telephone Employees Fishing Derby. Invariably, his big fish achievements rest with a fly tied some 60 years ago by his father, who was also an avid fisherman. At the time, fly tying materials were not as abundant as they are today, so his fly was simply spun from deer hair, which was readily found from the many hunters in those days. Fred ties the same fly today, with added eyes created by burning a short piece of monofilament at both ends. For larger eyes, he uses nylon "weed eater" cord as the base material and often colors the eyes with a black permanent marker pen. Fred tells me that small fish seem to ignore this pattern, but the larger trout attack it with gusto! Perhaps this is why Fred is so successful year after year at this fishing derby!

Materials

- Hook – Long shank streamer size 6 to 10
- Tail – None
- Rib – None
- Body – Mule deer hair
- Wing – None
- Thorax – None
- Head – None
- Eyes – Burned weed eater nylon cord to form "bulbs"
- Thread – Fine monofilament

Instructions

Before placing a hook in your vise, fire up a butane torch in a well-ventilated area. Cut a piece of weed eater nylon and, with a pair of needle nose pliers, touch the cord end to the flame to make a "bulb" at the end. Then cut the cord very short and burn a bulb on the other end. The nylon now connecting the two bulbs or eyes will only be about 1/8 inch long, just enough to show the eyes on both sides of the hook eye when tied in. After tying the nylon eyes across the hook eye, perpendicular to the hook shank, reattach your thread to the shank near the hook bend. Cut a piece of mule deer hair and spin it to the shank. Half hitch your tying thread just forward and spin on another clump of deer hair. As you continue spinning clumps of deer hair onto the shank, push each piece tightly back towards the hook bend. Keep spinning more clumps until the shank is filled right to the nylon eyes just behind the hook eye. Now the fun begins! Trim the deer hair carefully to form a long, slim dragonfly-like body. The deer hair will float, so Fred fishes this fly with a wet line, thus imitating a dragonfly nymph under water.

Fred McCrae, kneeling in a yellow jacket, at Doreen Lake

Fly 43: The Claret Lake Fly

A few years ago, my retired BC Hydro friend, Ray Hunt, suggested we try to locate a high-elevation lake west of Peachland. Neither of us had been there before, so we both inputted the coordinates into our GPS units and started off with high hopes of finding Claret Lake. It is a walk-in lake over 5,000 feet high, so the recent warm weather did not deter us. It did prove to be a challenge, not to locate the lake, but to find the secret ATV trail that makes the hike, with float tubes and all the necessary fishing gear, possible. To explain further, we first saw the lake through thick pine and spruce trees, with lots of blow-downs right to water's edge. It was certainly no place to try to walk in loaded with gear! To get on with the story, we knew there had to be an easier way in and finally reached a launch spot on the lake about four hours after leaving, fully double the time we had anticipated that it would take to reach the place!

Just before launching our float tubes, Ray asked me what fly he should use. As there was little surface activity, I suggested a wet fly like a Spratley or Woolly Bugger. He happened to pull a claret attractor fly from his fly-box and asked, "What about this one?" Without much thought I said, "Sure, give it a try, perhaps it echoes the name of this lake!" Well, to my delight and perhaps slight embarrassment, Ray proceeded to out-fish me five to one—and all bigger fish as well! I tried all of my patterns that worked well in the past, but those fish simply wanted the claret fly, the only one Ray had in his tackle box! After fishing, I borrowed Ray's rather beat-up fly to tie several copies at home. You can bet I will not visit another high-elevation lake in the summertime without bringing this fly, a pattern we will call the Claret Lake fly!

Materials

- Hook – Medium shank size 6 to 10
- Tail – Claret marabou with a few strands of claret angel hair and overlay of brown calf tail
- Body – Back half, brown calf tail; front half, wound claret marabou
- Rib – Front half thin gold wire
- Hackle – None
- Head – Gold bead
- Wing – None
- Thread – Fine monofilament

Instructions

The first step is to crimp the hook barb and slip a gold bead to the hook eye. Next, tie in a short claret marabou tail, mixed with a few strands of claret angel hair. Then, at about the halfway point on the hook shank, tie in a clump of brown calf tail, allowing it to flow back over the tail. At this point, attach a piece of thin gold wire. Next, select a long clump of claret chenille and wind it forward from the shank midpoint to the gold bead at the hook eye. Now rib this in three or four turns with the gold wire. Tie off, cement, and you have finished an excellent attractor fly for high-elevation lakes. Just ask Ray Hunt!

A high-elevation Okanagan area lake

Fly 44: The Fraser Sedge

Fred Kaltenbach worked for the BC Telephone Company for many years, in what many say is the still water capital of the world, Kamloops, BC. I also have had the good fortune to live and fish in Kamloops, although for a much shorter period in the early '80s. I have met Fred, and he recently sent me a description of one of his favorite Kamloops-area flies. It was given to Fred many years ago by Al Fraser, a skilled fly rod builder and fly tier of local fame. In fact, I still have a fly rod custom-built by Al Fraser when I lived in Kamloops. We do not know the original name of Al's fly, so we will call it the Fraser Sedge! Fred has always had great success with this fly in Kamloops-area lakes such as Roche, Frisken and Bulman Lakes.

Materials

- Hook – Medium shank size 6 to 10
- Tail – Black calf tail
- Body – Peacock sword
- Rib – None
- Hackle – Black
- Head – None
- Thorax – None
- Thread – Fine black

Instructions

Al's original fly is tied with black thread, but I prefer my usual invisible mending thread, because you can back wrap the body without discoloring or distorting the shape and this makes it stand up much longer! Start by tying in a short tail of black calf hair. Next, take a couple of peacock sword herls (the material from the eye of a peacock tail frond) and wrap a full body, hook bend to hook eye, just leaving enough room at the eye for the hackle. Here, make two or three turns of black hackle feather and tie off so the hackle slopes back a bit. Cement, and you have finished Fred Kaltenbach's favorite fly, the Fraser Sedge!

Son Allen on Roche Lake at the east side Forest Service campsite

Fly 45: The New Age Leech

When I drop into my local fly shop, Kelowna Trout Water Fly and Tackle, or slip over to West Kelowna to Wholesale Sports, I feel like a kid in a candy store with so many new products available. Whether these new age products catch more fishermen or fish is a debatable point! However, it is fun to experiment with new materials, and on occasion, they do really work. Such is the case with some fly tying items I purchased earlier this spring, including Stillwater Solutions' dark red-brown sparkle blend and Super Fly scud-back midge 1/8 inch chocolate strip. The latter material is likely meant for tying shrimp body backs, but I found a use for it in a new leech pattern that caught a beautiful rainbow trout just minutes into the water!

While on a July 1 trip to our Canim Lake summer camp, I thought I would test a new dinghy bottom and seat that I had fashioned to give my rubber raft stability. I took the craft to a small nearby lake and plied the oars a considerable distance to get past the weedy entrance. I put the new fly on a number 3 sink line with a fairly fine leader, and in seconds a good bright silver rainbow was leaping behind the boat! I cast the fly in again and had barely touched the oars when a mate to the first fish began taking line out as the reel screamed. Two fish were enough to feed our camp, so I turned the dinghy for shore, exceptionally pleased with my new fly. Let's have a look at this amazing pattern that I have aptly named the "New Age Leech"!

Materials

- Hook – Medium shank size 6 to 10
- Tail – 1/8 inch wide chocolate scud-back midge
- Body – Dark red-brown sparkle blend
- Hackle – Black short neck feather
- Head – Optional small gold bead
- Thread – Fine monofilament

Instructions

The scud-back material appears to have a stretchy, rubbery base that I felt would add terrific realism to a leech pattern. Tie in a length along the hook shank that projects a good body distance past the hook bend. Next, dub a body by forming a tying thread loop at the hook bend and insert about a 3-inch piece of rolled sparkle blend. Twist the loop many times and then wrap forward to the hook eye. After tying the dubbed sparkle blend off, make two or three wraps of short black neck hackle at the hook eye, taking care to force the fibers in a backward direction. As an option, I have also tied this fly with a gold bead for a head, and I have found both versions seem to work equally well! Try it, you will like it!

Bobbs Lake, east of Forest Grove

Fly 46: The Black Rabbit Leech

On one of my work postings to Prince George, I regularly met with other fly tiers as a member of the Polar Coachmen's Fly Fishing Club. One individual traveled all the way from his home on the Barkerville Road to attend meetings in Prince. As a sideline, he sold fly tying materials, so perhaps that was part of his motivation to drive so far! Capes of Jungle Cock fowl have long been banned, in an effort to preserve these wild birds, but this fellow offered Polar Coachmen members genuine capes at a bargain price. Yes, I succumbed and bought a jungle cock cape, which I still have today! Our fly that we will examine now is a flowing black rabbit leech, to which I have added jungle cock cheeks. Does it catch more fish? Well, it may not, but with the jungle cock cheeks, I tend to have more confidence in the fly, and that, I believe, results in more fish!

Materials

- Hook – Medium to short shank size 8 to 10
- Tail – None
- Body – Black mohair wool
- Rib – Medium copper wire
- Hackle – A single piece of crystal flash on each side
- Wing – Black rabbit strip
- Cheeks – Jungle cock
- Head – Peacock herl
- Thread – Fine monofilament

Instructions

Often near shore you will see very large leeches. However, I have found that a smaller leech fished in deeper water will often out-produce a large leech. That is why this fly is tied on a smaller hook than you might expect! Let's have a look at how I tie this fly.

Start by attaching a piece of copper wire to the hook shank and let it project past the hook bend. Next, wrap black mohair wool, hook bend to just before the hook eye. Follow up with spaced turns of the copper wire to form the rib. Now cut the underside skin of a black rabbit strip about as long as the hook shank. Depending on the length of the hair, it will flow back past the hook bend perhaps twice the hook shank distance, when firmly secured at the hook eye. I make a half hitch or two back along the hook shank to ensure the rabbit strip will stay fixed when attacked by huge trout! This fly doesn't have a hackle, but I add a single piece of green crystal flash on each side at the hook eye, flowing back about as long as the end of the rabbit fur. The jungle cock cheeks are an option, and if you have a cape, definitely tie in a jungle cock eye feather on each side at the hook eye. Finish the fly with a head of several turns of peacock herl. Cement, tie off, and you have a leech pattern that I have found produces really well in many Cariboo lakes!

Another awesome Cariboo Lake

Fly 47: The Wood Lake Kokanee

My Kelowna Royal Pine neighbor, Peter Bikicki, was new to fly fishing but certainly is a keen fisherman, especially so in the pursuit of kokanee, the smaller, lake-bound version of sockeye salmon. While I have caught kokanee on flies in the past, most fishermen use attractors such as a willow leaf gang troll with a worm or maggot. Wood Lake lies just north of my home in Kelowna and is known for sizable populations, in some years, of fairly large kokanee. Before leaving for a trip to Wood Lake with Peter, another friend suggested using an orange simulator-type fly with a fast sink wet line for these bright, lake-bound salmon. On sunny, bright days, I was told to try the same pattern in chartreuse or radiant pink, so, never to discard rumors about a good fly, I made several in all three colors. To my pleasant surprise, I found the orange pattern worked very well, with over a dozen strikes in two hours of fishing, pretty much keeping up to the fish attracted to Peter's hardware!

Materials

- Hook – Medium shank size 8
- Tail – Thin groundhog
- Body – Bright orange wool
- Rib – None
- Hackle – Short grizzly
- Head – Orange wool as part of the body
- Wing – Elk hair tied in mid body

- Thread – Fine monofilament

Instructions

Start with a thin tail of groundhog hair. I like groundhog because of the white tips, but more readily found gray or red squirrel is a good substitute. Next, form the rear body with orange wool tied fairly thin. Stop just over halfway to the hook eye, and at this point, tie a top wing of elk hair. Trim the butt ends of the elk hair, tie down firmly, and then continue wrapping the orange wool forward to the hook eye. Now, just a bit behind the hook eye, tie in a full grizzly hackle. Select a short fiber hackle and make about two complete turns. You should have a short length of the orange wool between this hackle and the hook eye. Cement, tie down, and you have finished a great kokanee fly. On sunny days, try chartreuse or radiant pink for the fly body.

Wood Lake, looking south to Winfield

Fly 48: The Mid Bead Nymph

So many of our still water flies are similar in make-up, yet subtle construction changes can sometimes mean the difference between a fishless day or not! This was the case when I was seeking late-season brookies near Kelowna this fall. For some reason, a small lake stocked with eastern brook trout produced only light taps using conventional flies, but a change to a new fly, at least for me, produced some amazing results. The fly we will inspect now is exactly what those brook trout wanted. How did I know? A simple change, for no other reason that it was a new fly in my hand-tied collection, produced vigorous strikes rather than light taps. So this fly recipe is definitely worth sharing!

Materials

- Hook – Medium shank size 8
- Tail – Brown or olive marabou
- Body – Back 3rd, brown dubbing, front half, orange chenille
- Rib – Mid body, oblong orange bead
- Hackle – Grizzly palmered through the orange chenille front half
- Thorax – None
- Thread – Fine monofilament

Instructions

Start by crimping the hook barb so that you can force a slightly oblong orange bead past the hook bend. Next, tie in a fairly thick tail of brown marabou. Just forward of the tail, wind brown dubbing of any kind or brown mohair to cover the back third of the hook shank, then slide the orange bead tight against this, approximately mid shank. I now tie in a thin grizzly hackle tip first at this point, followed by winding medium orange chenille from the bead to the hook eye. The final step is to palmer the grizzly hackle forward to the hook eye. Before tying off, as with most of my flies, I back wrap through the hackle to the bead and then back to the eye with my clear monofilament thread, taking great care not to distort the grizzly hackle. This provides strength to the fly, and the clear mono does not distort the body color. Whip finish and cement. For some unknown reason, the mid bead fly works better for brook trout than a fly with a bead at the head, at least for me!

A great Kelowna-area lake for brook trout

Fly 49: The Caverhill Nymph

Anyone who really enjoys fishing, whether with a fly or otherwise, will seldom fail to meet interesting people in their ongoing outdoor adventures. I believe it is inherent in our nature to relieve much of our daily life stress by just being outdoors! Yes, overcrowding on river banks when peak runs are on can lead to disputes, but in the main, most fishermen are congenial types who are willing to share many aspects of their fishing enjoyment. Over the years I have certainly met many fine individuals while on the water and also at gathering places, where discussions often revealed common fishing experiences. I have fished alongside such notables as Jack Shaw and Art Mikulak and listened to talks by Brian Chan when I was a member of the Kamloops Fly Fishers. My American fly fishing friend for many years, Steve Clements, has very kindly recommended a couple of flies tied by two of his well-known acquaintances, Peter Caverhill and Keith Findley, to share with you! Keith's fly is the Chromie in the Chironomid Chapter 4 section of this book, and we will now examine Peter's fly, the Caverhill Nymph!

Peter's fly, an offshoot of Kamloops fly tier Helen Peacock's classic fly, the Helen's Heller, proved to be a real winner on Dragon Lake several years ago. An October fishing trip to Dragon involving several well-known and adept fly fishers disclosed without a doubt on that day that the only productive fly for those huge rainbows was the Caverhill Nymph! So much so, I am convinced that this fly should be a basic pattern in your fly box! Peter has kindly given me permission to share the secrets of his pattern with you.

Materials

- Hook – 2x shank size 6 to 8
- Tail – None
- Body – Back 2/3, black mohair or similar, front 1/3, peacock herl
- Rib – Silver tinsel
- Hackle – Black, with very sparse clear flashabou added as an option
- Wing – The black hackle tied top and under side serves as a wing
- Head – Black tying thread
- Thread – Black

Instructions

Peter's original fly was tied with a mohair body, but modern materials now add a bit of colored flash, as in the picture of the Caverhill Nymph above, which is one of Peter's hand-tied flies. Start by fixing a length of medium silver tinsel to the hook shank for later use as a rib. Then wind black mohair, hook bend to a full 2/3 distance to the hook eye, followed by three or four turns of the tinsel to form a rib over the mohair. At this point, tie in the black hackle on both the top and underside of the body so that the rib clearly shows through from each side of the hook. Now complete the forward body with peacock herl and finish the fly with a tapered head of black tying thread wraps. I guarantee you will be in famous company using this fly, with my sincere thanks to Peter Caverhill!

Peter Caverhill releasing a fine Thompson River rainbow

Fly 50: The Big Yellow

I have always found excitement in big fish lakes; more so small, hidden lakes that harbor at least a few monster trout. I feel fortunate that within an hour's drive of our Canim Lake summer camp, there is such a lake! A couple of years ago, I saw a picture of a rainbow that was just over 13 pounds, fly-caught in this lake. While I have not yet captured a trout that big, I have discovered, through some trial and error, a fly that is quite effective in persuading those huge fish to strike! Allow me to share that pattern with you!

Materials

- Hook – Medium shank size 6 or 8
- Body – Bright yellow chenille
- Rib – Medium gold wire
- Hackle – Brown pheasant tail on each side with a green crystal strand
- Head – Thick peacock herl
- Thread – Fine monofilament

Instructions

This fly, which I call Big Yellow for the large fish it attracts, is quite easy to tie. I believe perhaps the extra attraction of this fly is the strand of crystal flash in the side hackle or horizontal wings. Start by securing a length of medium gold wire to the hook shank and let it project past the hook bend. Next, tightly wrap bright yellow medium chenille hook bend to hook eye. Follow up with spaced wraps of the gold wire to form a rib. Now, one at a time, attach a small clump of pheasant tail feather to the side of the fly, flowing back from the hook eye about as long as the fly body. The next step is key; tie beside the wing hackles a single strand of green crystal flash, also as long as the hook body. Finish this big fish fly with a generous wrap of peacock herl to form a fairly large head. Cement, tie off, and you have tied a fly that large trout in my secret lake just love!

Big trout await in this small Cariboo lake

Chapter 6:

HOW TO TIE MY FAVORITE STEELHEAD/SALMON FLIES

Fly 51: The Purple Bitch

I first met Steve Clements in a roundabout way many years ago, through a coffee break discussion in the Prince George Telephone Engineering Office. Joe Bernat, an Outside Plant Technician, maintained a summer RV trailer at Tachick Lake, near Vanderhoof, BC. Steve and his wife, Pat, who reside in Seattle, Washington, frequently used the Tachick Lake RV Campsite as their RV base in order to fly fish area lakes and streams. As all fishermen do, evening campfire visits soon brought Joe and Steve together on a first-name basis. One evening, Steve asked Joe if he knew of any other keen northern area fly fishermen and Joe replied, "One of our engineers, Don Haaheim, just lives and breathes fly fishing!" An invitation to visit Steve at Tachick Lake soon followed, and the rest is history. Over the years, Steve and I have fished many BC rivers and lakes, where I have come to appreciate Steve's fly fishing enthusiasm, expertise and unwavering conservation ethics.

Steve is an adept fly tier and has created patterns for both trout and steelhead. A pattern called the Clements' Bitch evolved from careful observation of Hobson Lake leeches that huge trout in that South Vanderhoof lake gulped with abandon! He has also tied a similar fly for steelhead, which he calls the Purple Bitch. It seems that this fly is equally successful for those huge river rainbows as the related leech fly is on lakes and is definitely worth a close review.

Materials

- Hook – Mustad 38890 or equivalent size 1
- Tail – Purple marabou, part of wing flow back
- Body – Wrapped purple marabou
- Rib – None
- Wing – Purple Marabou
- Head – Black tying thread, option peacock herl
- Thread – Black Uni size 0/8

Instructions

Steve's steelhead fly is not hard to tie; just ensure the marabou wing flows back along the hook body. Start by tying in a body of purple marabou fairly thick. Next, in two or three progressive steps, add a purple marabou wing, with the last tie near the hook eye. Complete the fly with either a black tying thread head or green peacock herl. The picture of Steve with a fly-caught steelhead on the Kispiox River proves the worth of his creation!

Steve Clements releasing a huge Kispiox River steelhead

Fly 52: The Vedder Chum Fly

The Vedder River, near Chilliwack, BC, must be one of the most productive rivers located near a large urban center, in the world. At different times of the year, all five species of native West Coast salmon spawn in this magnificent river! As well, starting in December and continuing for the winter months, steelhead inhabit the river system. In September and as late as November, you often find good quantities of spring, pink, coho and chum salmon in the river. In early October, I journeyed from my Kelowna home, having made reservations at the Vedder River Campground, for a few days of fishing just prior to our Thanksgiving weekend. Among the regular fishermen, I was surprised to see almost two dozen people all the way from Italy, here to enjoy the salmon fishing. In fact, when I arrived, I was immediately helped by a gentleman from the next RV spot to guide my trailer safely into my camping place. When I offered my thanks, I found out that he could not speak much English, yet we did find a way to communicate rather well in what you might say was an international fisherman's language! He and his group had heard of the great Vedder fishing and had recently traveled all the way from Italy to test the river's numerous salmon.

I mention this because the first two evenings I fished the Browne Road pool where the Italian group also fished, being an easy walk downstream from the campground. When I arrived, they had already assembled in a long line at the head of the pool, casting their drift outfits into the fast water at the far bank. And catch fish they did, both large springs and some coho, with much laughter among the group as a lucky angler with a hooked fish ran downstream trying to hold the salmon in the swift water. Most often, the fish was lost, but they did beach a few, releasing the springs and wild coho but retaining an occasional hatchery coho. I chose to fish just below the group, knowing that this stretch of water also held fish. I had taken both my drift rod and fly rod, so I opted to fly fish just to see if I could hook a salmon to show the visitors that fly fishing could also work in this river! I was about to give up and switch to a drift float rod when I had a solid hit on my polar bear fly. The salmon felt heavy but did not jump, so I suspected that it may have been a chum salmon. As the fish made a couple of strong runs, the fishermen nearby stopped fishing to watch the action. "Chum," I said to the onlookers, as I slowly worked the large fish nearer to the shore. Sure enough, I saw that it was a male chum salmon of about fifteen pounds, which I carefully released with a pair of pliers, not wanting to get near its sharp teeth even though I was using a barbless fly. This fly, which I call the Vedder Chum fly, is quite similar to the famous Mickey Finn, a time-honored pattern that has a layered bucktail red and yellow wing and a silver body!

Materials

- Hook – Nickel Eagle Claw steelhead L1197N size 4
- Tail – None
- Body – Red #12 Uni-mylar
- Ribbing – Thin silver wire
- Hackle – None
- Head – Black tying thread with a dot of orange dimensional fabric paint
- Wing – A few strands of light green crystal flash mixed with orange polar bear, then overlay with white polar bear hair
- Thread – Light monofilament and black for the head

Instructions

Attach short lengths of both the red Uni-mylar and thin silver wire to the hook shank. Wind the Uni-mylar starting part way down the hook bend to the hook eye, followed by the silver wire in tight evenly spaced wraps to form the rib. Next, mix a few strands of light green crystal flash into a clump of orange polar bear hair and tie in at the hook eye so that it flows back over the shank to form a wing. Overlay this with a smaller clump of white polar bear hair. I usually finish the wing with a couple of strands of crystal flash over the white layer of hair. The final step is to wind a black head with black tying thread or floss. You can also use a large dab of orange or yellow fabric paint on both sides of the head and then make a black pupil for a more realistic eye. Tie off, cement, and you have finished the Vedder River Chum Salmon fly!

Vedder River, just downstream from the Browne Road pool

Fly 53: The Faithful Woolly Worm

The green woolly bugger that we previously tied is one of my favorite trout flies, but a similar fly, the woolly worm, is also one of my favorite steelhead flies! As December rolls around and as all true fishermen desperately try to avoid the commercial hype of Christmas for as long as possible, thoughts of steelhead come to mind. Strong, bright silver fish begin entering the lower mainland rivers such as the Vedder, and the more northerly streams such as the Kalum and Bulkley are well into their steelhead season.

Many years ago, when I first lived in Prince George, I drove out to the Bulkley for a late fall steelhead fishing trip. I had the good fortune to meet a local angler from Houston, Art Dyksdra, who on that day, was the only other fisherman in the vicinity. He kindly offered to take me and my small dog, Pepper, out in his 14-foot aluminum boat in order to reach several pools that were inaccessible by direct wading. I gladly accepted his offer and, furthermore, he fished the water through each pool that we tried after me! He was using a black woolly worm on a sink tip line. I did not land a single fish that day, even though I had first crack at the holding water, but Art, following me, landed and released 3 beautiful steelhead! Since that day, I have been a fan of the black steelhead woolly worm!

Materials

- Hook – Mustad black 36890 size 2 to 8
- Tail – Radiant pink yarn
- Body – Black Chenille

- Ribbing – None
- Hackle – Fine grizzly hackle tied in palmer style
- Head – Optional turn or two of peacock herl
- Wing – None
- Thread – Fine monofilament

Instructions

For fast water, wind in a few turns of lead near the hook eye. I usually have both weighted and unweighted woolly worms in my fly-box! After attaching your tying thread to the hook shank, tie in a short tail, no more than 1/4 inch, of radiant pink yarn, although you can experiment with many different colors. Then secure a short fiber grizzly hackle, tip first, at the tail. Before wrapping the hackle forward, attach a piece of medium black chenille to the hook shank and tightly wind it forward to the hook eye and half hitch it in place there. The final step is to carefully wrap the grizzly hackle forward to the hook eye and tie off. If you use invisible thread as your tying material, it is possible to wind the thread back and forth through the hackle to make the fly hackle much more durable for the rigors of casting and fish strikes! A turn or two of peacock herl at the head is optional to complete this very effective steelhead fly.

Bulkley River, east of Telkwa

Fly 54: The Steelhead Sack-fly

It was late morning on the Morice River. I had been diligently casting for steelhead since dawn. Even though it was only early September, at daybreak ice crystals had formed in my rod guides. Now it was approaching 11 a.m. and the sun was beginning to get very warm. I knew there were a few early run steelies in the river, but up to that point, not a nibble for all of my hard efforts! I decided to change to a sack-fly as I worked my way down to the tail of a long run not too far up from the confluence of the Bulkley River. The sack-fly swung into fairly deep water as it straightened out from my long cast across the river. Then it happened! A silver bright steelhead was leaping clear of the water, hardly a fraction of a second after I felt a savage strike! The sack-fly was solidly hooked in the corner of the steelhead's mouth and held for the duration of a short but violent battle.

A Prince George fly tying mentor, Steve Head, had proclaimed that the sack-fly was an excellent steelhead fly, but I had serious doubts in my mind. It looks dull and uninteresting to me and it is made from an old burlap sack, so how could it be a good steelhead fly? However, after that morning on the Morice, I became a believer.

Materials

- Hook – Mustad steelhead 3666 size 4
- Tail – Red embroidery thread or kip's tail
- Body – A single strand from a brown burlap gunny sack
- Ribbing – Optional thin gold wire

- Hackle – Red squirrel tail
- Head – Thin peacock herl
- Wing – Red squirrel tail
- Thread – Black and fine monofilament for body back wrap

Instructions

Attach your tying thread to the hook shank and tie in a short tail of red embroidery thread. Then wind a single strand of burlap, pulled from a brown gunny sack, from the hook bend to the eye and tie off. The burlap body can be strengthened by back wrapping fine monofilament thread to the hook bend and back to the eye. Next, attach a piece of red squirrel tail at the hook eye and tie it in so that it flows back over the burlap body of the fly. This wing should be not much longer than the bend of the hook. The throat hackle can then be easily tied in by flipping the fly in your tying vise and, with the hook upside-down, simply attach a small piece of red squirrel at the hook eye, about 1/2 the amount used for the wing, and allow it to flow back fairly tight to the fly body as you cinch the hackle down. Finish the fly by wrapping a few turns of peacock herl at the hook eye. Whip finish, cement, and you have just created a steelhead fly that may well produce some very pleasant results for you!

The Bulkley River in early fall

Fly 55: Dave's Rabbit Intruder

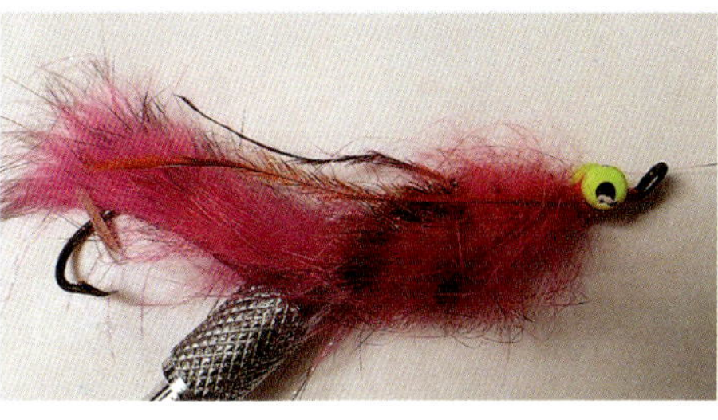

I have found fly movement is key for more steelhead hook-ups, and rabbit fur often is a prime ingredient to create this movement. My trap shooting friend, Dave Upper, is a solid believer as well. Dave lives at Bowser, BC, with his lovely wife, Diane, who does approve of Dave spending many days in steelhead season fishing those great Vancouver Island rivers! Dave specializes in an intruder type steelhead fly that uses rabbit fur as the principal material. He calls his fly the Rabbit Intruder, a large fly that casts well with the Spey outfit that Dave prefers for his steelhead outings.

Materials

- Hook – Black salmon size 2 long for the body, Gamakatsu 1 or 1/0 for the stinger hook
- Tail – Part of the rabbit strip wing
- Body – Purple pearl chenille
- Rib – None
- Hackle – None
- Head – Lead dumb-bell eyes painted green with black pupils
- Wing – Pink rabbit strip, several strands of crystal flash, and then two outside strands of orange ostrich herl
- Thread – Fine monofilament

Instructions

Before starting on the fly body, loop a piece of fly line backing or strong braided material to the larger salmon hook shank. Dave makes about a 1/2 inch loop for the trailing stinger hook and doubles back the braided line on the salmon hook shank, cinching it throughout its length with tying thread. He then cements the entire shank and lets it dry before proceeding to the next step. When dry, tie in several strands of crystal flash to the salmon hook shank and let it trail about two inches past the hook bend. Over this, wind the pearl chenille just behind where the lead eyes will be, to the hook bend. Next, attach a pink rabbit strip near the hook eye and let it trail back about as long as the strands of crystal flash. Now tie in a strand of orange ostrich herl on each side of the hook shank. The next step is to solidly figure-eight a dumb-bell eye set just back of the hook eye. Dave then likes to paint the eyes green with black pupils and also covers the tying thread between the eyes with orange paint. I am sure you can experiment with different colors and still have a very successful steelhead fly! To complete the process, cut off the salmon hook at the start of the bend, leaving your tied material in place on the hook shank. The last step is to push the loop through a stinger hook eye and around its bend so that you can snug the trailing hook up tight. Now just try to keep those steelies away from this fly!

Dave Upper holding a Spey-caught steelhead, soon to be released

Fly 56: The Campbell River Pink

In early September, I told my trap-shooting friend, Dave Bartee, that I had recently caught a couple of pink salmon at the mouth of the Oyster River on the east coast of Vancouver Island. "That's nothing," said Dave, "I fished the Campbell River just up from the Gold River junction and caught 60 pinks using a fly in three days! And here is the fly to prove it," he went on to say! I certainly was impressed and asked numerous questions about his equipment and how he managed to land and release so many salmon. He explained that he didn't move along the river, but stayed with his back to a large rock, casting into the current so that his fly was swept into a good holding area for pink salmon. He used only one fly, which we will examine here, and it did the job admirably. In fact, Dave said that after three days, his arm was very sore from all the action. When I asked what the name of this magic fly was, he said that he didn't know, so we will call it the Campbell River Pink Salmon Fly.

Materials

- Hook – Tiemco 5262 size 8
- Tail – Pink marabou
- Body – Radiant pink chenille
- Ribbing – None
- Hackle – Radiant pink neck hackle
- Head – Pink bead

- Wing – Thin radiant pink hackle
- Thread – Pink

Instructions

Crimp the hook barb and slide a pink bead through to the hook eye. Next, cut a clump of pink marabou and make a fairly short tail. Then attach the radiant pink chenille to the hook shank and wind forward from the hook bend to the bead just behind the hook eye. The final step is to wind a couple of turns of pink neck or saddle hackle immediately behind the bead. As an alternative, you can tie in a throat hackle and wing separately. Tie off, and you have finished a first-class pink salmon fly!

Further to Dave's successful pink salmon story, I have also caught many pinks while wading the ocean surf near the mouth of the Cluxewe River using a pink and white fly. It seems that fresh-run pink salmon are up and ready to strike on more than one type of radiant pink colors used to create a productive fly pattern!

Fly casting for pink salmon at Cluxewe, Malcolm Island in background

Fly 57: The Tube Fly

The old saying, "You are never too old to learn something new," certainly proved true to me fairly late in my fly tying career. I had heard of tube flies for several years and some of their inherent advantages, such as the ability to use short shanked hooks, for not only better hooking but also improved retention of fish. As well, the hook can easily be changed if the point becomes dull or if a different size is preferred. The other day I decided to give these tube flies a try at my tying vise, and I soon found that tube flies are relatively easy to tie! You can purchase metal or plastic tubes designed just for this type of fly but I thought: Why not use spare materials in my basement workshop to give it a go? I therefore cut a red spray tube from an empty WD40 can into several pieces about 3/4 inch long. I knew that I needed a holder to extend the tube past the jaws of the tying vise, so I simply clipped off the eye of a long streamer hook and pushed the straight end tightly into the tube. Presto, a holder that held the tube securely for the tying steps ahead! A needle of the correct size would probably also do the job. Tying the materials to the tube as explained below was then relatively easy.

Materials

- Hook – Short shank steelhead size 2
- Body – Red plastic tube about 3/4 inch long
- Ribbing – None
- Hackle – White polar bear beard

- Head – Green tying thread
- Wing – Underlay white polar bear followed by a green layer, then topped with blue polar bear
- Thread – Thin monofilament and green for the head

Instructions

Push a clipped eyeless hook or darning needle into the red plastic piece of tube. After securing the hook or needle in your vise, create a long beard hackle by tying in white polar bear hair near the far end of the tube. I found that the red plastic tube could be twisted upright for this first step, then down to complete the wing on top. The tube wing is composed of three layers of polar bear, starting with a white under-layer. Next, tie in a second layer of green polar bear hair and complete the wing with an overlay of blue polar bear. The final step is to change your tying thread from fine monofilament to a green rod winding thread and wind over the wing cut ends to form a fairly large green head. Oh yes, the hook! Simply select the leader size that you intend to use and tie a needle knot onto a size 2 short shank steelhead hook. Push the free end of the leader through the tube (after removal from the vise), then a double surgeon's knot to tie that piece of leader to your main leader and line! Notice how the tube fly can slide up the leader, but water pressure will keep it snug to the hook during the retrieve. By varying the materials/colors, you can create patterns for both salmon and steelhead!

Tube fly water on the Vedder River

Fly 58: The Sockeye Pigtail

Like 2010, 2014 was the year of the sockeye! Perhaps the DFO estimate of the Fraser River return was not up to an earlier prediction that the sockeye run would be greater than four years previous, but after three trips from Kelowna to the lower Fraser, I was convinced that summer 2014 was a sockeye fisherman's delight! I had the good fortune to be invited to fish the river with my friend Dave Hesketh, using his Alumaweld jet boat, two trips in August and one in mid-September. Even the September trip produced many nice sockeye using our bottom bouncing technique, not exactly fly fishing but still a lot of fun!

Dave's son Dan, who now lives with his family in Terrace, BC, developed a hook set-up for sockeye and also spring salmon, which I have tried with great success.The forward part is basically a yarn fly, which I frequently use as a Spey casting pattern.

Materials

- Hook – Black Matzuo or Gamakatsu size 4/0 to 1/0
- Tail – Pigtailed corky with a small stopper bead
- Body – Small amount of yarn, color optional
- Head – Needle knot
- Thread – 30 pound test monofilament

Instructions

Author holding a nice Fraser River sockeye caught on a yarn fly

The trick to tying the corky pigtail fly for sockeye is making a needle knot (sometimes called a nail or barrel knot) on the hook shank. In fact, I do not use a needle to pull the leader end back through the loops, but rather a short tube cut from an old WD 40 red nozzle spray tube. I push the leader end through the hook eye about 10 inches past the hook bend, with the short tube parallel to the hook shank. Using my left-hand forefinger and thumb to hold the first turn in place, I wind about nine turns back towards the hook eye, then thread the leader end back through the tube. The next step is to pull the tube out from the loops, while keeping the loops from springing free with your right thumb and forefinger. Pull the leader end tight to secure the knot and give it a final tightening by pulling hard in both directions. You should now have several inches of leader end projecting past the knot. First, thread a medium corky, then a small bead onto the end of the leader. Tie a tight double granny knot so that the bead and corky can slide just past the hook bend and trim the excess close to this knot. I like to burn the trimmed end with a lighter to ensure the holding knot will not come apart and thus lose the corky. Now the leader, just past the hook eye, can be pushed back to create a loop or opening at the shank side of the hook eye. Insert a short piece of yarn—to me, color does not matter, but Dan likes peach with a bit of red yarn ahead of the peach. Pull tight, and you will find the corky helps to keep the hook from snagging on bottom rocks and thus more salmon hook-ups!

Fly 59: The Bill Shea Oiler

My friend Bill Shea from Kenmore, Washington, was a lifelong fly fisherman and superb fly tier! Unfortunately, Bill recently passed away, but he has left us with a legacy of hand-tied flies created in the colors of many North American professional and college sport teams. Such an example is the Bill Shea Oiler, a steelhead fly tied in the colors of one of our Canadian National Hockey League teams. I happen to be a hockey fan as well as a fly fisherman, and Bill's Oiler fly therefore has double appeal for me! The fly has movement and bright colors for murky water, so I know it will appeal to all avid steelheaders!

Materials

- Hook – Alec Jackson 2000 SKU series
- Body – None, blank hook shank
- Hackle – Short sparse white hen
- Head – Heavy black tying thread
- Wing – 1st layer or underlay, royal blue marabou, next, 6 strands blue crystal flash, 3rd layer or overlay, orange marabou
- Thread – Fine monofilament and then black for the head

Instructions

This is probably my favorite long flowing 360-degree wing of three layers. Start by tying in royal blue marabou near, but leaving a short space from, the hook eye. Ensure that the marabou flows back equally above as well as below the hook shank. Next, overlay the marabou with about six strands of blue crystal flash the same length as the marabou. Now spin orange marabou as the third layer, also flowing back equally above and below the hook shank. The next step is to make one or two turns of very sparse, short white hen hackle close to the hook eye, covering the wing tie down spot. Finish the fly with heavy black tying thread to create a black head. You have created a great steelhead hockey fly, although the team it represents has had a hard time winning in the past few years. Perhaps the performance of the fly for steelhead will be much better? It is a snap to tie with no tail or body, just leave the hook shank bare!

Dave Hesketh and son Allen on great salmon and steelhead water

Fly 60: The Coquihalla Orange

Tommy Brayshaw was one of British Columbia's well-known fly fishing pioneers. He was born in Yorkshire, England, in 1886 and moved to Canada in the early 1900s. Not only is he known for developing a series of flies, but he was an acknowledged artist and carver of trout and steelhead. In fact, in 1998, Canada Post issued a series of commemorative fishing stamps including Brayshaw's Coquihalla Orange! His fishing career took him to many of BC's famed trout lakes, such as Knouff Lake, in its early '30s heyday. Brayshaw retired to Hope and became very familiar with, at the time, one of BC's most productive steelhead rivers, the Coquihalla. He created five steelhead flies just for fishing this river: the Coquihalla Red, the Coquihalla Black and Silver, the Coquihalla Silver, the Coquihalla Orange Dark, and the Coquihalla Orange. Tommy Brayshaw passed away in 1967, but if he were alive today, he would no doubt be disappointed to witness the steelhead decline in his favorite river. We can only hope that restoration efforts will gradually bring back the Coquihalla River to its former glory! Let's have a look at Tommy's famous fly.

Materials

- Hook – Salmon size 2 to 8
- Tip – Fine silver tinsel
- Tail – Golden pheasant tippet
- Butt – Black Ostrich herl

- Body – Rear half, orange yarn; front half, dubbed polar bear underfur
- Rib – Gold tinsel
- Hackle – Throat hackle red saddle
- Cheek – Jungle cock (optional and not shown above)
- Wing – White polar bear over orange polar bear
- Head – Black
- Thread – Fine monofilament (the original used black thread)

Instructions

Begin by tying in a short tip of fine silver tinsel at the hook bend. Next, make a tail of golden pheasant tippet, although golden pheasant crest can also be used. A turn or two of black ostrich just at the start of the hook bend forms a butt. Before starting on the body, tie in a piece of gold tinsel just ahead of the butt, as this will be used for the rib. Now wind bright orange yarn from the butt to halfway up the shank and continue with dubbed orange polar bear underfur, if you have it. If not, complete the body with the orange yarn. At this point, wind the gold tinsel in spaced turns hook butt to near the hook eye. Next, tie in a fairly short throat hackle of red hen feather. The wing is next, in two stages: an underwing of orange polar bear, and then an overwing of white polar bear hair. A final touch before cementing is a few turns of black shiny thread to form a head. In the days when summer steelhead flourished in the Coquihalla River, Tommy Brayshaw used this pattern with good success, and there is no doubt in my mind that his fly will still catch fish!

The Coquihalla River in late summer flow

Chapter 7:

HOW TO TIE MY FAVORITE DRY FLIES

Fly 61: The Elk Hair Sedge

During a late June or early July evening, approach many of the smaller Interior lakes where oil slicks from 2-cycle outboards have not decimated the natural caddis populations, and you will be treated to a fly fisherman's delight. Rainbow trout wildly leaping and slashing at newly emerged sedges that are scampering across the surface in preparation for a flight to shoreline trees. This is the time that you must be equipped with a floating fly line and a good supply of dry flies, preferably sedge imitations such as the Mikulak or Goddard sedge. I prefer to tie a Mikulak type pattern with elk rather than deer hair, as I find that elk stands up much better to the violent strikes of large trout.

Materials

- Hook – Medium shank size 6 to 10
- Tail – None
- Body – Mottled green and blue wool or green dubbed seal hair
- Wing – Upper leg elk hair
- Head – Round clipped hair, optional dark thread winding
- Hackle – Short brown saddle (option)
- Thread – Fine monofilament

Instructions

I blend the green and blue wool for the body so that both colors show, almost as if the fly body was ribbed. In some lakes, the sedge bodies are various shades of green, often lighter than one would expect, and I have also seen grays and brown as well, so do not hesitate to experiment with different shades for the sedge body. You can either wrap the wool or dub it on with a twisted loop in your tying thread. Again, I prefer invisible mending thread, as I can create a lumpy effect along the fly shank without changing the color of the body. The next step is the key to my elk sedge. I use several pieces of elk hair and start by tying the first piece just forward of the hook bend. The next piece is tied just ahead of that; keep repeating the process until you tie in the last piece near the fly head. Each piece of elk hair is cut to length, so that together they form a uniform wing over the body. An option is to not bother with measured lengths and trim to a uniform length later. Invisible mending thread or fine monofilament will allow you to tie in several pieces of elk hair along the hook shank and still show the body wool color! The last step, as an option, is to wind in a full brown hackle at the hook eye, tie off, cement, and you are finished. I have experienced superb dry fly fishing with the elk sedge in Community, Ernest, Hyas and Lac des Roches, to name a few lakes. Cast to areas where fish are rising and try to skitter the fly in your retrieve by applying short but fast pulls on the fly. Then watch out for that explosion as a wild rainbow tries to tear the fly apart!

Island near the west end of Lac des Roches, good dry fly water

Fly 62: The Dark Mayfly

Most mayflies are shades of gray or sometimes brown, but at least one of our BC Interior lakes has a prolific spring hatch of dark, almost black mayflies! A late May trip I made to Jimmy Lake featured very threatening weather; in fact, shortly after lunch, a sprinkle of rain developed from the darkening clouds. To my surprise, dark mayflies began to hatch, and as the rain came down harder, more and more mayflies braved the elements! I had only gray mayflies in my fly box, which the large Jimmy Lake rainbows steadfastly refused, although they were vigorously slashing at the emerging black mayflies! I decided then and there never to be caught again without a supply of dark mayflies. The fly we will examine now is a product of that interesting Jimmy Lake day.

Materials

- Hook – Short shank dry size 8 to 14
- Tail – Two turkey tail feather strands
- Body – Thin black foam strips
- Rib – None
- Hackle – Black saddle
- Wing – Two turkey feather tail pieces with an upward curve
- Thread – Fine monofilament

Instructions

Select two long, thin, turkey feather tail fibers with an upward natural curve and secure them to the hook shank. The tail can project back and upward twice the length of the hook shank. Then wrap a thin strip of black foam hook bend to hook eye, as this material will make the fly much more buoyant. Note, you can make your own foam strips if you buy thin foam sheets, available in various colors at most fabric shops. Next, carefully tie in two pieces of turkey tail feather, selected for an upward curve, about 1/3 distance from the hook eye. This wing set should project well above the body but not as long as the tail. Wrapping the black saddle hackle next, mainly ahead of the wings but also a few turns behind, will help to keep the wings upright. Cement, tie off, and you have finished an excellent dry fly for Jimmy Lake rainbows in the rain!

Jimmy Lake at the BC Forestry campsite

Fly 63: The Amazing Humpy

Early spring, a favorite time of year for many fly fishermen, is also a period when weather can be extremely variable. My observations have been that dependable insect hatches in reasonably large quantities do not happen until consistent weather conditions occur, especially those regular warm, sunny periods around midday and early afternoon. Perhaps this is so because evolution has conditioned better insect survivability during warmer and more stable environmental conditions. But in spite of some very wild weather in early spring, hatches sometime occur in surprising quantities, enough so that suddenly huge trout will be crazily gulping surface insects and send you into shivers as you hurry to change to a dry fly! And how woeful is the fly fisherman who has not come equipped with at least some dry flies to try to match the hatch. I have found that the Humpy fly, tied in a wide range of sizes, can be an answer to the puzzle of how to catch early season trout on a dry line. It is similar to the old standby, the Tom Thumb, but the Humpy body can be tied in any number of body colors, and that is a good part of the secret to better match the hatch when they occur on those early spring days.

Materials

- Hook – Medium shank size 6 to 22
- Tail – Deer or elk hair, which is actually part of the fly back
- Body – Various colors (red, green, blue, brown etc.) of wool, seal hair or mohair etc.

- Hackle--Deer or elk hair which is part of the fly back, then optional turns of grizzly
- Wing--The upright part of the hackle described above
- Thread--Fine monofilament or black

Instructions

The great variation in hook size as well as different body colors often gives you an advantage over having more exact copies of insects, whether mayflies or sedges. In other words, if you have a good supply of Humpies of different colors and sizes in your fly box, you may not need any other type of dry fly to successfully catch fish when those surface hatches develop. Start by either dubbing a body if you are using seal hair or winding a piece of wool or mohair to form a fairly thin body, hook bend to hook eye. Then select a clump of either deer or elk hair at least twice as long as the hook shank. I prefer the durability of elk, but sometimes the grayer appearance of deer hair is a better match for mayflies. Place the clump with the larger cut end at the hook eye and parallel to the hook shank, so that the hair tips are well past the hook bend; i.e., the cut ends also project past the hook eye the same distance as the tail. Now gently wind your fine monofilament thread back and forth to secure the hair above the body so that the body color underneath is plainly visible, hook eye to bend and back to the eye and cinch it there. Trim off the splayed larger ends of the hair at the hook eye. Then fold over about 3/4 of the hair at the hook bend and bring it back to the hook eye, where you must securely cinch it down. This creates an upright hackle or wing. If the original hair piece was not long enough, cut another hair hunk, and also secure it at the hook eye, fold over at the bend, back to the eye and cinch here, creating the upright front wing. You can neaten the cut ends at the eye with a few turns of black thread or floss. The last step, as an option, is to wind in a couple of turns of grizzly hackle at the hook eye, tie off, cement, and you have just completed one of the most versatile dry flies that exists, the Humpy!

Doreen Lake, excellent for evening dry fly fishing

Fly 64: The Thompson Hopper

My family and I spent two wonderful years in Kamloops back in the early '80s; my wife and kids enjoyed the convenience of smaller town living and I appreciated the exceptional fly fishing available in the area! When the lakes slowed in August, I still managed some exceptional dry fly angling in the South Thompson River below Walhachin. The Thompson rainbows, some very large, did not object to grasshopper winds that blew the insects into the river at that time of year. I devised a dry fly that worked quite well using a foam component for extra flotation. Let's have a look at this creation, which I call my Thompson Hopper.

Materials

- Hook—Long shank dry size 4 to 8
- Tail – None
- Body – Back half, yellow wool; front, brown mohair
- Rib – Brown rod thread size D
- Hackle – None
- Wing – Elk hair
- Legs – Pumpkin barred rubber Sili legs
- Head – Yellow foam
- Thread – Fine monofilament

Instructions

Start by tying in a length of brown rod thread (size D is great) to the hook shank for later ribbing. To help fly flotation, I now cinch in a piece of foam to the hook shank in tight wraps. Next, overlay the foam with yellow wool hook bend to about 2/3 way to the hook eye. Follow up with spaced turns of the brown thread over the wool to form a rib. At this point, I tie in a rubber leg on each side of the body and put a single knot in each leg near the end. In those early years I did not have the products that are available now, such as White River Sili Legs, but why not use the more modern material now? Then finish the front of the body with turns of brown mohair. In the next step, I like to use elk for the wing for better durability, but deer hair will do if you are not an elk hunter! The last step is to cut a piece of yellow foam about 1/8 inch wide and tie it in at the hook eye and back far enough to cover the large ends of the elk wing. Tie off, cement, and you have created an excellent river hopper fly!

The South Thompson River, downstream from Walhachin

Fly 65: The Caddis Floater

Early July is sedge or caddis time in many of our Southern Interior lakes. Big sedges that scamper across the surface, leaving a very visible wake for sharp-eyed trout ready to pounce! Many of us have been frustrated when sedge imitations do not stay high on the surface after becoming waterlogged from casting or, if we are so lucky, repeated strikes from large trout! George Barron of Kamloops has solved this problem by tying a sedge imitation made of flex-foam that is guaranteed to float. You may ask why trout would strike at a foam wing creation, but, when a thick caddis hatch is underway, I have found that the fish often lose their sense of caution!

Materials

- Hook – Long shank size 4 to 8
- Body – Small tan or olive flex-foam strip
- Hackle – Brown neck hackle feather
- Wing – Brown or gray folded flex-foam cut to resemble the caddis wings
- Thread – black

Instructions

The first step is to find a craft or sewing shop that sells thin sheets of colored flex-foam, not more than 1/8 inch thick. They are inexpensive, so pick up several colors, including gray, green, yellow, black, and brown. The body and head of this fly are made from a tightly wrapped strip of flex-foam, so cut a piece of thin olive foam about 1/8 inch wide. Attach it near the eye and secure it back to the hook bend in a straight line with your tying thread, then tightly wrap the foam forward to the hook eye and tie off. The wings are next, and this requires some scissor work on a brown or gray sheet of thin foam. Measure the length of the wings by allowing it to project about 1/4 inch past the bend. Cut sort of triangle out of the foam, wide at the tail and narrow where you will attach it near the hook eye. Fold it over and tie the narrow end near the hook eye with about 1/8 inch of the foam showing for the head. Then wind a few turns of brown hackle feather to represent legs just behind the head. A tip is to cement the fold in the wing so it will stay close to the body, and you can make a small razor cut, not all of the way through, on the center of the wing so that the fold will better stay in place. A few turns of black tying thread will finish the head. George guarantees that this fly will float under any conditions!

The northeast end of Johnson Lake, good caddis water

Fly 66: The Brown Black Ant

I have not often witnessed flying ants settling in trees and, with the aid of wind, dropping into lake water deep enough to stir trout into a feeding frenzy. One such occasion did occur at Opacho Lake, a bit south and east of Prince George, BC. I happened to be anchored near the south shore of this small but pretty Cariboo lake when I noticed a lot of surface activity a short distance away. I quickly lifted anchor and, as I neared, I could see the water was just rippled with slashing trout! Why? Flying ants had migrated to a large alder tree partly overhanging the lake edge, and a reasonably brisk shore breeze was blowing some of the migrants out into the lake. As well, a few ants seemed to be falling directly below the tree after they had clipped off their wings. No matter to the gorging rainbows, they happily gobbled up any ant that hit the surface, or at least it seemed that way! At the time, I did not have a good ant pattern so I tied on a black gnat dry fly of similar size and did have a couple of hits. I vowed then not to be caught without an ant pattern, and after the action had died down, I rowed in to the leaning tree for a closer look. Most of the larger ants that I had seen in the past were all black, but this time there appeared to be some brown color associated with these insects.

Back at home, I tied some floating ant patterns, half brown and half black, and even when those rare ant migrations were not evident, I did have some success fishing this fly, enough so that it is a worthy pattern to have in your fly-box! I also ignored the wings of a freshly fallen ant, and this did not seem to matter to our prime targets, hungry trout!

Materials

- Hook – Short shank size 10 to 12
- Body – Initial wrap of black holographic tinsel, then rear brown and front black foam strips
- Hackle – Middle brown, front black
- Wing – None
- Thread – Fine monofilament

Instructions

These ants are not large, so begin with a 1x dry fly hook and wrap it, hook bend to eye, with black holographic tinsel. This will give the fly just a bit of attractive sparkle from the underside. Next, cut two short 1/8 inch wide foam strips, one brown and the other black, from your craft shop sheets. Cinch down the brown strip at the hook bend and again at mid shank of the hook. Continue with the black piece mid shank, then tie it down at the hook eye so that both foam strips are left with humps. The last step is to wind a few turns of short brown hackle in the middle and, again, short black hackle at the hook eye. Cement, tie off, and you have created a great fly for those few occasions when flying ants hit the water and send the fish into a frenzy!

Opacho Lake, a Cariboo gem

Fly 67: The Haig-Brown Steelhead Bee

Roderick Haig-Brown was a mentor for me in my early fly fishing days. I have read all of this prolific author's fishing books with great interest! He is without a doubt a British Columbia fly fishing pioneer with the extraordinary talent of putting his fishing experiences into very eloquent words. Roderick was born in Sussex, England, in 1908 and passed away on October 9, 1976, in Campbell River, where he and his wife, Ann, had made their home by the namesake river for many years. He became thoroughly familiar with the Campbell River flow in all seasons, not just for trout, but also for steelhead and salmon. Roderick devised many flies to catch all types of fish in his home river, one of which is the steelhead bee.

I am proud to say that Haig-Brown was a dedicated conservationist, a fact recognized by the BC government, which named a provincial park after him! The park, which displays a wealth of information, was established in 1977. If you want to make a visit, early October is an excellent time. Starting from Chase, BC, drive about 10 kilometers east along the Trans-Canada Highway, then turn north on the Squilax-Anglemont Road and follow it for about six kilometers to the provincial park sign on the right. The location, near the outflow of the Adams River into Shuswap Lake, is a huge spawning area for sockeye salmon, especially every four years—as happened, for example, in 2010, 2014 and hopefully in 2018.

I still have a letter sent to me about salmon life cycles signed by the master, dated August 17, 1970, with his address at 2250 Campbell River Road. A very meaningful memento, indeed! I feel that it is very fitting to end my favorite fly collection with a Roderick Haig-Brown pattern as a salute to the true dean of British Columbia fly fishers!

Materials

- Hook – Salmon dry size 4 to 10
- Body – 1/3 brown, 1/3 yellow, 1/3 brown large chenille or spun and clipped deer hair
- Tail—Brown squirrel or moose hair
- Hackle – Brown neck hackle feather
- Wing – Dark brown squirrel or moose hair bent slightly forward
- Thread – Fine monofilament (original black or brown)

Instructions

Start by tying in a tail, medium length, of brown squirrel or moose hair. A mix of both is fine. The body is completed with 1/3 yellow, 1/3 brown and 1/3 large chenille, or if you want a better floater, use dyed deer hair spun and clipped to length. A wing is then formed with dark moose hair tied so that it slants slightly over the hook eye. The fly is finished with a brown hackle feather wound both in front and back of the wing. According to legend, Roderick hooked and released many summer steelhead with this pattern!

A provincial park dedicated to the master, Roderick Haig-Brown*
Ed Note: A new entrance just west now exists called "TSUTSWECW"

Chapter 8:

SAFETY FIRST

I hope you can see from my comments associated with tying my favorite flies how much I enjoy fishing, especially when using my hand tied flies! I still try to get out of doors fishing as often as possible, sometimes too much, according to my dear wife, Lois! Yes, I hope the excitement of seeing a strong fish rise to a dry fly or sighting large trout or salmon just waiting for a wet fly to slip past their nose will not interfere with your safe water sense! However, we fishermen can get caught up in the excitement of the moment and forget about the old adage, "safety first." Of the hundreds or even thousands of times I have been outdoors fishing, whether in rivers or lakes, I have often seen other fishermen not wearing life jackets or other flotation gear. I will admit that I have been guilty of this in the past, but I am now convinced it is not the wisest thing to do!

Allow me to relate two experiences that I have had in my fishing career. One early morning, on the fast-flowing Vedder River at Tamahi Rapids, I was standing on a rock about 8 feet out from shore. As luck would have it, I hooked a large coho and tried to jump back to shore using an intermediate rock. Everything would have been fine except that the salmon gave a strong pull as my foot left the original rock and the other foot landed in water rather than on the next rock! Under water in the fast-moving current I went, still doggedly holding on to my rod, with a fish adding to the pull downstream! Fortunately, about 20 feet downriver, the current swept closer to shore and I was able to regain my footing, although drenched from head to toe! Yet somehow I still held onto my fishing rod, and about 100 feet downstream, I landed an 8-pound coho—only to find it was a wild salmon and had to be released! I have a floater fishing vest, but guess where it was? Sitting on shore beside my backpack—not much good when you are being swept downriver wearing chest waders! I do, however, use a belt to cinch up the waist of my waders and this slows the water entry if you decide to take a cold water swim! Luckily, my good friend Dave Hesketh, who was successfully fishing by a large streamside rock upriver from me, had a complete change of dry clothing in his camper to augment the items that I did not have!

Dave Hesketh, coho fishing in fast water at Tamahi Rapids

The second unwanted water experience occurred on June 13, 2017, when my fishing partner, Al Kouritzin, and I explored a new lake west of the small town of 100 Mile House. Terry Kehler, a retired Royal Bank manager, once worked at 100 Mile and knew of an excellent brook trout lake in the area. With Terry's description, Al and I eventually found, with a little help from a grader operator, the neat Forestry Campsite at this lake.

We quickly launched Al's aluminum 12-foot car topper, but after a couple of hours dragging flies without a touch or even seeing a fish rise in the water, we decided to try fishing chironomids with strike indicators near shore. Again, nothing was happening, so our next plan was to slowly row near shore weeds in an effort to spot any fish in the crystal clear water. We saw lots of pollywogs, sedges, damsel flies and the like; then, after some 10 minutes of rowing, there they were! Near the bottom in about 10 feet of water, I saw about two dozen brook trout, perhaps two to eight pounds estimated size—in fact, it reminded me of a school of salmon!

We quickly anchored, and when we could see the fish between gusts of wind, we hurriedly cast chironomids over the slowly moving trout. My chironomid, a Producer described in Chapter 4, was too small for me to see when it sank near the bottom, but whenever a fish turned near where I estimated my fly to be, I gave a tug on my floating line. Wham! I was suddenly into a good brookie, and luckily the fish fought near the surface, allowing me to land a fine male brook trout that weighed just over 6 pounds! I did have a second strike, but that fish stayed deep, tangling in weeds, so you might call it a conservation release.

I was rather surprised that the fish school did not scare away as we repeatedly cast over them. However, wind gusts prevented us from seeing their slow and steady movement, so to get a better view during brief calm spells, I stood up on the front seat of the boat. Not wise, because when Al also stood up, boom, over we went, with everything we had spilling into the water. My green floater fishing vest was only a few feet away and fortunately, even though I was wearing a rather heavy mackinaw shirt, I was able to quickly swim to it. Al also was not wearing a life vest, but he too was able to secure his floater and wisely headed for shore about 100 feet away. Seeing that holding onto my floater vest with one hand kept me from sinking, I turned the aluminum boat upright from the back end, then slowly worked my way to the front to lift the anchor. Gathering things as I went, including the floating oars, I kicked towards shore with my free hand on the boat rope. By then Al had made shore and, after taking off his drenched clothes and shoes, swam out to help get the boat in! My, but a boat full of water is heavy! By tipping the boat from the middle on one side, we slowly managed to empty the car topper at the shore.

I certainly learned a lot that day. Fly rods, with their hollow cores will sink reel end to the bottom, but the tips will be straight up. In our case, the tips were only about 6 inches under water, so all were retrieved when we rowed out to the spill area to salvage as much gear as possible. My Nikon digital camera was in a black Samsonite case with a knitted shoulder strap. Was I ever surprised to see the strap floating upward from the bottom in about 10 feet of water, possibly air contained in the strap weave? Anyway, by hooking the reel of a 9 foot fly rod through the strap loop, we managed to pull the camera case to the surface! Then, to my utter amazement, I found the camera still worked after about 30 minutes under water! In fact, the following pictures were taken after the camera was retrieved. Now what about my prize brook trout? There it was, settled in the weedy bottom some 10 feet down! Another gift, as Al managed to hook a rod tip in the big trout's open jaw and gently lifted it to the surface, so the fish was not lost! However, we could

not retrieve a few items, but we do consider we are much wiser fishermen for the experience. Forever on, I will wear a floating device when on the water, and I do recommend that to all of you fly tiers who venture out in pursuit of our wonderful finny friends!

Al Kouritzin, after an unplanned early June swim

The 6-pound brook trout that was caught twice!

Acknowledgements

One of the many reasons that fly tying is so enjoyable is the great friends that one meets while pursuing this hobby. Many of the fly patterns in this book are not my creations but are credited to other individuals. Sharing all kinds of information is a common occurrence among our fishing fraternity, and for that I am extremely grateful! Allow me to mention a few folks below to whom I owe special thanks for their contributions to this book.

1) My longtime friend and fishing partner, Al Kouritzin of Kelowna, who has given me many ideas from his steadfast research of fly patterns.
2) Prince George's Dale Ruth, together with his wife Lucille, have created many interesting fly patterns, including Fly # 41, the Mallard Concord. Thanks Dale and Lucille.
3) One of my longtime friends, who in my early Prince George years provided untold fly fishing encouragement, is Steve Clements of Seattle, Washington. Steve has kindly given me permission to use several of his copyrighted photographs in this book.
4) A classic British Columbia fly is the Caverhill Nymph, and Peter Caverhill has provided me not only with his original hand-tied flies but also great background information about his awesome creation!

5) Keith and Cleo Findley have also provided the amazing story about landing a huge Dragon Lake rainbow trout on a tiny size 14 chironomid! My sincere thanks to Keith and Cleo!
6) One of the best salmon fishing friends I have is Dave Hesketh, who lives on a Christian Valley ranch with his lovely wife, Bev. I continue to be amazed at Dave's ability to catch river salmon, especially when the fishing is slow for the rest of us mortals!
7) Another retired commercial fisherman is my Vancouver Island friend Dave Upper, who has become a modern steelhead expert. Dave has created many steelhead Spey fly patterns that work wonderfully well!
8) My late friend Bill Shea of Kenmore, Washington, personally knew Doctor Spratley, of Doc Spratley fly fame. Before his passing, Bill shared a treasure of fly tying information with me, and I am indeed grateful for such generosity!
9) After moving from my second stay in Prince George to Kelowna in 1986, the usual chores of finding new doctors, dentists and the like had to be undertaken. Friends told me that Al LaBounty was not only a good dentist, but also an expert fly fisherman and fly tier. As luck would have it, Al accepted me as a new patient and, while I cannot say a visit to the dentist is much fun, I gained a wonderful amount of fly fishing information during these "open mouth, another tooth repair" sessions! I am indeed grateful for this sharing, Al, and also at no extra charge!
10) Besides the folks mentioned above, I wish to thank Tony, Joe, Rich, George, Ray, Fred, Barry, John, Mark, Irv, Roy, Ken, Ted, Les, Kirsten, Marge and many others who have helped to create fly patterns outlined in this book. While I have not mentioned everyone by name, I do offer my thanks for sharing their gift with fly fishermen and women everywhere!

A fly fisher's dream: a Bulkley River photo by Steve Clements

Epilogue

Steve's photo of the fly caster in an early-morning Bulkley River mist, as featured on the cover, was my inspiration for the following verse.

Early Morning River Mist**

I gathered up my fishing gear,
And drove the miles to river bright,
A warm and cheerful rustling sight!
To be away from city strife,
Was giving me a lease on life,
To cast again for fish so strong,
I know that's where I must belong!

I met old friends late in the day,
No time to put a rod in play,
And there at streamside we set up,
A camp in time for evening sup!
With stories told of past delight,
Grand fish grew large with every bite!
A campfire warm to stir the heart,
Of fishing pals right from the start!

But dawn arrived too soon for us,
We staggered up at last to cuss,
At fog so thick we could not see,
The clearing edge where stood a tree!
But then we heard o'er river roar,
The splash of fish our hearts did soar,
To race upon the water fast,
And in the mist began to cast!

I could not see my steelhead bee,
Land near to where the fish might be,
But full of hope I cast the fly,
And quickly time went sailing by!
Then all at once my greatest wish,
Had rod in double bent with fish,
I know of no more better sight,
Than steelhead bright of pure delight!

I then held tight the rod in hand,
As steelhead raced the stream so grand,
And high in air the fish did leap,
How could I hold that line and keep,
The fly tight in the steelhead lip,
When such pure strength it tore at tip,
To show to all in awesome light,
A great display to feel such might!

RELATED TITLES

Fishing the Canadian Rockies 2nd Edition is an updated, revised and comprehensive guidebook to the lakes, rivers and streams of the Canadian Rockies. The area covered by Fishing the Canadian Rockies, extends from the Canada-U.S. border in the south, through Jasper, Switzer and Mt. Robson parks in the north. Both the Alberta and British Columbia sides of the Continental Divide through the Rockies are covered.

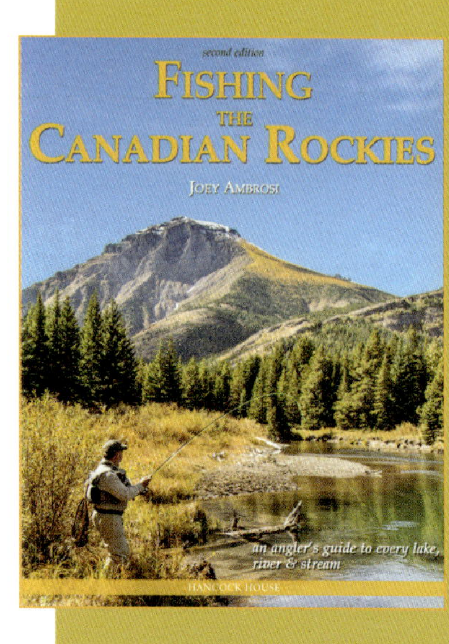

Fishing the Canadian Rockies

Ambrosi, Joey

978-0-88839-425-5 [paperback]
978-0-88839-349-4 [epub]
8½ x 11, sc, 248pp

$39.95

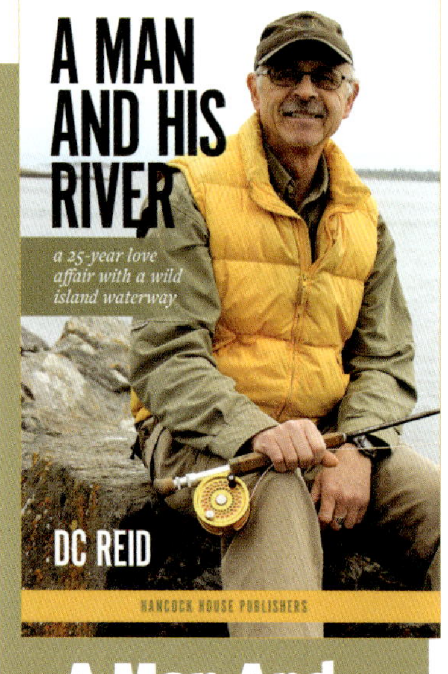

A Man And His River

Reid, DC

978-0-88839-728-7 [paperback]
978-0-88839-734-8 [epub]

5½ x 8½, sc, 256pp

$24.95

A 25-Year Love Affair with a Wild Island Waterway

A Man and His River is a love story, and a story of personal journey set on the banks of the Nitinat river on Vancouver Island. It is about the inherent and universal feeling of being near flowing water and the experiences of nature and wildlife that share the banks. This book is also a summary of the author's lifetime of fishing Vancouver Islands 123 watersheds and the pursuits of its diversity of salmon and trout.

The Tactical Secrets of Lake Fishing

This straightforward fishing guide was written for the average fisherman. The focus is on tactics and a handful of secrets that keep fishing simple and enjoyable. These secrets are really a set of easy and logical processes that answer three basic questions: Where should I fish? What do I fish with? When do I fish? The key is in the relationship between trout and their changing ecology, and understanding how complex behavior is really a set of simple and predictable patterns. Ed looks at the basic physiology and instincts of fish and ends up with proven methods for catching fish. No other book so vividly related behavioral science to angling tactics.

Trout Fishing

Rychkun, Ed

978-0-88839-338-8 [paperback]

5½ x 8½, sc, 120pp

$16.95

The 12 Basic Skills of Fly Fishing

Peck, Ted & Ed Rychkun

978-0-88839-392-0 [paperback]
5½ x 8½, sc, 42pp

$11.95

Authors Ted Peck and Ed Rychkun cut through the mystique and complexity surrounding fly fishing and come up with the twelve basic skills needed to understand and enjoy the engrossing art of fly fishing. Here they present a breakdown of fly fishing basics for the beginner. Covering topics such as the selection of equipment, holding a fly rod, mastering the roll cast, stripping the line, handling and landing fish- this book covers everything the beginner needs to know.